Ga

How to cultivate and fu   ...ess, heart intelligence
and soulful wisdo,   Ju gather your family,
friends   .J colleagues

Sonya Wilkins

Sonya Wilkins

Sonya is an holistic consultant, artist and mother whose goal is to
create ways for people to cultivate a better connection between
their authentic selves and others in this busy world.
She combines wisdom from her holistic training and people
development background to break through 'the dust of every day
life' and bring you interactive ways to enlighten
any type of gathering.

Sonya worked at Astrazeneca Pharmaceuticals for 10 years
in various people development roles until 2007 when she
retrained as an holistic therapist.

Today she offers a variety of personal healing and transformation
therapies, from Reiki, to MBTI® coaching and therapeutic art
tuition through Bristol Reiki Healing Arts.

Contents

Dedication ~ For You

You have it too? That uneasy feeling that we've started to lose something important in life...the ability to talk, really talk and listen to the ones we love?

For all those Mums and Dads who worry their children will never experience those traditional family dinners talking about the day they've had, like they once did growing up.

For all those who want to see into the hearts and minds of those they love, whether family, friends or acquaintances.

For all those who want to open the door to their Soul and to understand what makes their inner spark perpetuate and shine.

The door has just opened...start to Gather Insights with those you love!

My Wish For You

I would like to invite you on a journey of discovery. A journey where you will re-awaken the ability to listen and learn about those people you share your life with. To see clearly into their character, personality, feelings and ultimately get a glimpse into their Soul; the essence of what makes them who they are.

Even if those around you are 2 years old or over 100 there are gems of beauty to be found in the moments when we all choose to share our hearts and minds. This book provides a fun and light hearted framework where families and friends can ask simple yet provoking questions around the dinner table, camp fire, even in the car on long journeys, while walking the dog, or huddled around the kitchen table over tea and cake!

These questions act as catalysts for insight and revelation. You will be amazed at what your children will share and how they share it. This process of revelation will bring joy when you realise you are seeing them truly. Every little morsel of reply will nourish the family and bond members together in laughter and revelation. You will see things in your friends you never knew before, you will enrich all your relationships…just from simple questions!

Yes, this book is simple, certainly not rocket science, but there is a subtle significance within the pages. I am hoping that by compiling the questions that opened my own eyes to the ones I love, (and even got my teenage son so engaged we couldn't stop him sharing); that it will generate a ripple in your lake of love and increased self awareness and one-ness.

You can simply work through the questions in sequence or dip in and out. You can throw a dice and choose questions at random, marking them off as you go, or ask people to choose a number from 1-52 at random. There are 52 questions, so you can arrange to dine together once a week over a period of a year and play the game once each time. Or, you can blast as many questions out in a sitting as you like! Go with the flow!

My hope is that this little book brings you insight, revelation and joy. That it ultimately helps to bind you to your loved ones, growing soulful wisdom along the way and you come to realise how powerful it can be, to be truly present with the ones we love...

"In our busy world and frequent face to face disconnection, this gem of a guidebook offers fun and fresh tools to nourish relationships and deepen the connection between those with whom we spend our daily time. Even just by reading the questions we get to realise we perhaps don't know the insides of our family's minds as much as we first thought! Sonya offers a beautiful blend of grounded wisdom, child friendly magic and soul-nourishing awareness in her unique range of questions for enquiring into the hearts and minds of loved ones. She manages to skilfully weave in her holistic expertise in an accessible way for added insights and self awareness."

Gina Schofield ~ Channel & Energy Healer at Guidance From The Stars

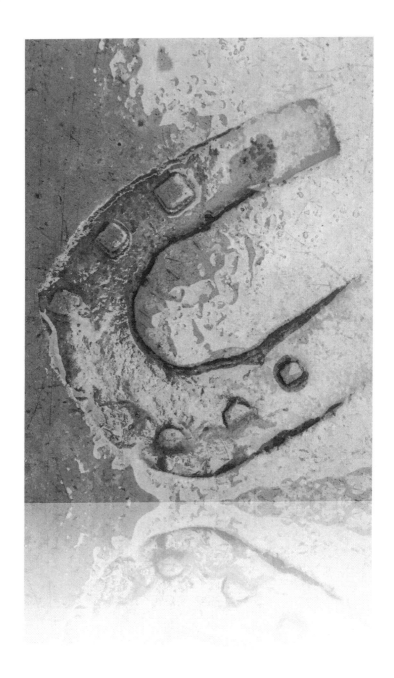

Foreword
By Richard Addison

I love quirky, interesting books. I particularly love quirky, interesting books that entertain adults and children on long journeys in my slow, arthritic Toyota. I'm quite sure that this book has many uses on many occasions but for me, entertainment in the car is the vital one. And this book does the job beautifully.

I've tried all possible methods to entertain infants, youths and adults in the car - playing cricket games using cars, buses and lorries for runs, and a game involving yellow cars although I've forgotten exactly what to do with the yellow cars.

I've tried asking my passengers to think up 101 'hilarious' ways of impressing your neighbours on the cheap, such as putting a dustbin lid on the roof and telling your neighbours you've had Sky installed. We dreamed up 11 ideas, well short of the 52 in this book.

I've tried a competition to think up the most ridiculous (bogus) facts about fruit. For example, The Beatles sang about 'Strawberry Fields Forever'. This was a better title than the original idea 'Raspberry Open Spaces for a Very Long Time'. This didn't take off.

And during a journey to Wolverhampton, we tried to make up a joke for every letter of the alphabet. For example, E is for Egypt, and here's the joke: When the workers were building the Pyramids, if they got a bad back they went to see a Cairo-practor. This also didn't take off.

However this book is different. It makes you think. It can even make you sound intelligent. It is the perfect book for healthy debate and will brighten tedious getaways.

Finally I have the thing for my passengers. Much better than my ideas!

~

Richard Addison, author of FINDING ANOTHER LINDA, has written comedy for film, TV and radio. He is an award-winning presenter and lectures regularly on writing for film and TV. Richard is the author of 14 published books including dinosaur companion books for Spielberg's epic film The Lost World. Richard has been a model. He has been a press officer for the Government. He is a descendent of Edward the First and related to Joseph Addison, writer and founder of The Spectator. Richard is currently writing the screenplay based on his novel FINDING ANOTHER LINDA.

Preface

I am so grateful to Elizabeth Gilbert for writing her book 'Big Magic' because although the idea for 'Gathering Insights' came to me while at the dinner table with my own family, I was inspired to take action and write it because I read 'Big Magic' on a holiday in 2017. The golden nugget I took from her book was the suggestion that ideas are like entities in their own right; they visit us in our minds, and we have a choice whether to embrace that idea and take action, or not. If we take too long to decide, quite often the idea can literally journey to someone else, and then it becomes their idea instead. So, when I realised there may be something special hidden in this simple idea, I knew this was my chance to give birth to it - I wasn't going to let it go. If I hadn't read 'Big Magic' I don't think I would have had the courage and foresight to do something about it, so my thanks go to Elizabeth for inspiring me to take action and look at the world of ideas, creativity and inspiration in a whole new way.

Of course creating this book took a little time, as I am both a Mother and Step Mother to four children, a ceramic artist making and selling my own pottery and a healing consultant offering support to people on their path to increased self awareness. Even so, the idea was planted, and as my connection to the idea of creation and my interest in spiritual development started to merge in late 2017, the birth of this little book seemed timely. So, in between these different flavours of my life, I made sure I fed this little idea with enough nourishment to keep it alive until it was the right time to launch it on its journey into the world.

With the support of my best friend and husband, Neil, the spur of imagination from my children, Max and Macy, and lots of question testing with Ellie and Hannah, my step daughters…and not forgetting a little help from the powers above, here it is!

I am grateful for the many teachings I have received in my life so far, because they have become the ingredients I could inject into the supporting chapters in this book. It's amazing how, once your world is opened by a little knowledge, you suddenly realise how little you really know. I find that exciting, I know that if we are all willing to look, really look and understand each other better, we can open our eyes to new dimensions and ultimately shift our destiny as a united whole.

Many years ago, I worked as a people development consultant in a large organisation. I was part of a unique group helping people work better in teams, offering 1:1 coaching and insights through my qualification in *MBTI Psychometric testing and other personality tools. I was able to help people understand their personality preferences, allowing them to communicate more effectively both at work and in their personal lives. Often these sessions opened a little window into peoples' perception of themselves and others, allowing them to take the first step towards self awareness and an understanding about how our communication styles influence others.

I was then drawn to look into the world of energetic healing and I became qualified in Reiki level I and II in 2009. This shift in my own perception of the world supported me through a challenging transition in my personal life and I experienced first hand the impact of this new found knowledge. Many other holistic qualifications and teachings followed, enhanced by my art practice which continues to be my meditation and food for my soul. I have now come to a point where I am applying all this rich learning into my own life, using intention to create my reality, and consciously choosing words as conduits for positive change and spreading kindness. Through this awakened knowledge and understanding I continue to learn how to create new positive habits in my life, unplugging stagnant patterns of behaviour and ultimately training my mind so allowing the wisdom in my heart and soul to be expressed. My goal is to be aligned with my soul contract, acting as a conduit for wisdom and kindness for those who seek it.

This little book is a beginning, and one that I hope opens up a little window in your world of people and experiences. It can help you to see what is around you, how you respond and how you have influence within your world. One universal law says that we attract what we project. So the very fact that you are reading this now must mean that on some level you are ready to open your own treasure chest of potential. It's no co-incidence that you've bought this book. So, enjoy the adventure in front of you and open your eyes to all the 'wonder-full' people around you with all their diversity and how they and you influence each other on this adventure called life.

I have structured this book so that you can easily dip into the questions and use them in different ways. Either methodically working through them (one per week if preferred) or randomly selecting them as you go along. The questions form the practical part of the book where you will gain most of the delicious learning. I have personally experienced real revelations about my own friends and family's characters and perspectives on life while using these questions at gatherings. It is often a real awakening in my understanding of them, and what's more, that understanding changes with each interaction using the 52 questions; they can in fact be used again and again as peoples' answers change over time. As we know, nothing in life stays the same - the only certainty in life is change, and we all change too…constantly transforming and evolving as people. Therefore, so too will our answers to these questions!

Alongside the questions I have supplied some prompts, equivalent anecdotes, or alternative phrases that can assist you when explaining some of the more 'adult' questions to a younger audience. I've purposely sprinkled the list of 52 questions with seemingly simplistic questions and then alternating with more in-depth questions, so there is a variety for all ages. Interestingly, you will find some of the more simplistic questions are often the most enlightening for us adults, particularly when answered by our innocent and wide-eyed children!

I have also given you some supporting material for further reading and reflection in the later chapters of this book. I've chosen some topics that stood out for me as important yet easy to absorb. The first topic covers the therapeutic aspects of communication and some scientific evidence to support why it is so important to laugh and talk. I then go on to discuss the power of sharing problems, or 'getting things off our chest', the importance of active listening and how this is different to normal 'hearing'; how this can improve our relationships and ground our own state of mind. I look at the animal kingdom for more perspective on how our hearing has evolved over time and how it could transform in the future. I discuss the power of language and words, and how we can shape our reality with their careful and conscious use. I contrast this by discussing the significance of body language and reading visual cues; how our bodies and their movements provide additional information about how we really feel and what we think compared to the words we actually speak. This dovetails with my final chapter on aura intelligence, introducing the idea of seeing beyond our existing five senses. Using intuition as a guidance tool and expanding our awareness beyond our physical being.

How To Gather Insights

When I started formulating the questions that would ignite my Family's attention I wasn't sure how many I would come up with; and believe me, with every time we gathered together for a meal and chat, there were, and continue to be, more questions suggested for a sequel! However for starters, I thought 52 was a logical number because as a Mum I know how hard it is to get everyone around the table with all the modern day demands and distractions like after school clubs, homework, gym classes and tech!

I felt once a week was realistic. Of course I'd like you to beat that but let's start off making this a special time where for one night a week the mobiles are put in another room or turned off, the meal is prepared (maybe prepared as a family or group - if you're feeling brave!) and the table is made to feel loved because it is being used as it should be - for enjoying each other's company over wholesome food. When we are facing each other or at least adjacent, we are able to observe and really listen to each other, so connection starts to grow. There is also something wonderfully authentic about sitting around something, whether it be a table, or fire. The experience, I believe, takes us back to our roots, or origin and those days of tradition and sharing.

This book can also be used on car journeys - handy for those long ones! Or really anywhere where you are together with people and you take a moment to connect. It's so easy to pop the little book in a pocket and dip into the questions.

You may like to be methodical. You can work through the questions in order, ticking them off as you go. Or you may like to use them randomly but still marking them off as they are completed. But remember, each question can be used more than once…as you'll be amazed how you get different answers on different days from the same people. Our life experiences mould our responses to the world all the time. So actually this book can be used as a framework to see how peoples' perceptions change over time…interesting!

If you want to make the book more interactive with little ones then you can use a dice thrown twice to create a number correlating to the questions in the book. For simplicity, you can agree that the youngest person chooses first or you can simply ask people to flick the pages with their eyes closed, and blindly place their finger on the page to choose their question. You could even use a blindfold and explain that often our unconscious chooses things for us and this is more likely to happen when our normal senses are switched off. By blind folding, we are inviting our intuition to choose the questions we would find most useful to discuss. Or just choose a number between 1-52 at random!

The subsequent chapters are designed to give you a bit more information to chew on. By using 'Gathering Insights' you will have utilised a number of skills in order to connect with the members in your group. But you may have missed some.

These chapters describe ways in which we can 'Gather Insights' more effectively, learning to really hear, see, and interpret what the people around us say in answer to the questions. They actually make up some of the essential skills I believe we need to hone in order to be effective, communicative, and emotionally intelligent human beings.

You may even choose to read these supporting chapters first before working through the 52 questions so you are primed with knowledge; or you may decide to work through the book in the order it is presented, maybe repeating the 52 questions to see what difference your new found knowledge will bring.

Trust that you will use this little book at the right time, as it can be pulled out at any time, for all time!

Enjoy!

It's Time...

To Gather Insights...

52 Insightful Q's

Please also reference the 'Helpful Prompts' for these 52 questions in the next chapter by matching up the corresponding question numbers. It will help you to explain the questions to younger members of the group, and extend some of the questions further, giving more clarity and depth.

1. **What do you like most about each of the other people in the group? Go around the table and share one attribute about each person that you respect and wish you could have yourself and explain why.**

   Aim to share something about their character, personality or it could be a physical attribute; a positive quality that is unique to them. After you have shared your answer for everyone in the group, take it in turns so everyone in the group has shared with everyone else.

2. **If you were the leader of a small community of people, what 5 rules would you require your people to live by and why?**

   You may need some time to mull this one over and think about your rules, so allow reflection in your group and whoever is ready to go first can kick off! Take it in turns to answer this same question so everyone in the group has shared with everyone else. This one is sure to encourage discussion!

3. **What do you think LOVE is? What does it mean to you?**

It's been said that 'Love is not a feeling, it is an action'. Perhaps it's a choice we all have and in making a decision to love, and taking loving actions, we can grow and increase the feeling of love. Take it in turns to answer this same question so everyone in the group has shared with everyone else. Watch out for body language with this exercise as talking about love, certainly for adults, can be an emotive subject, and give important clues as to how that person is feeling currently in their relationships. Ensure the group is supportive if emotions become overwhelming, particularly if memories of passed loved ones emerge. Read the chapter about 'Visual Cues' if you'd like to improve your observational skills while reading people's reactions.

4. **If you were a food, what food would you be and why? If you could then invent a new food what would that be? Look like? Taste like? Feel like? What properties might it have?**

Describe how it would be packaged and branded and sold to people. Take it in turns to answer these same questions so everyone in the group has shared with everyone else. You can have some real fun with this one...it will also get your appetite going so make sure you have a meal prepared or some nibbles handy!

5. **What is the most important lesson you have learnt so far in your life and what have you done differently since as a result?**

One of the most important things you can do in life is to make mistakes because we often learn more from mistakes than successes; the second most important thing is to make sure you learn from them! Take it in turns to answer this same question so everyone in the group has shared with everyone else.

6. **If you could be a superhero who would you be and why? What would your powers be? What would your superhero outfit be like?**

   Tell us everything about your superhero! Take it in turns to answer these same questions so everyone in the group has shared with everyone else.

7. **Some believe 'Mother Nature' is the custodian of all plants and animals: is the conductor of earth, sky, water and fire and is the 'Soul' or 'Heart' of our living planet Earth. What do you think Mother Nature thinks about our human existence on her planet and how we treat her? What would you do differently?**

   This question is deliberately open, so people can express their different views and ideas on what is an important, popular and sometimes contentious topic. This is a great opportunity to debate and also educate the younger people in a group about environmental issues. Take it in turns to answer these same questions so everyone in the group has shared with everyone else.

8. **Share 2 statements (it can be anything) that start with 'I Think' and 2 statements starting with 'I Feel'. Now describe the difference in them and where you think they both were generated in your body. Which style do you prefer using and why? Which is most important to you, thinking or feeling?**

   This question is a great indicator of personality preference. It can show how we make decisions, based on logic or feelings. Both are equally valid but have different styles and can affect how we communicate with others if two different styles collide. So it's really important to 'go inside your body' when you say your statements and describe the difference in where the response is coming from when you share the statements. Take it in turns to answer this same question so everyone in the group has shared with everyone else.

9. **Which piece of music or song best describes who you are. If you can, play a few minutes of it, sharing it with the group or singing it!**

   Take it in turns to answer this same question so everyone in the group has shared with everyone else - you can have a very entertaining time with this one, and it often generates lots of laughter!

10. **What is your Soul? Where is it? What feeds your Soul?**

   This is a deep one, but really interesting to see how everyone responds! Take it in turns to answer these same questions so everyone in the group has shared with everyone else.

11. **If you were emigrating to live on the planet Mars and could only take 3 personal items with you, which 3 things would you take and why?**

   Take it in turns to answer this same question so everyone in the group has shared with everyone else.

12. **What are the top 5 values you think are most important to teach the people you are responsible for?**

   If you are a parent, you can describe the values you would teach your children; If you are a mentor, coach or manager in your job you may choose to describe the values you teach those people in your team or organisation; If you are a child you may like to choose the values you would teach the children in the year below you at school, or younger siblings or pets! Take it in turns to answer this same question so everyone in the group has shared with everyone else.

13. If you could press a button and transport yourself anywhere in the world whenever you wanted, where would that special place be for you?

Share some memories associated with that special place and why it is important to you. Take it in turns to answer this same question so everyone in the group has shared with everyone else.

14. When have you felt you were connected to something bigger than yourself?

Describe what it was, where you were, how it felt and what you think was going on to make you feel this way. Take it in turns to answer this same question so everyone in the group has shared with everyone else.

15. If you were a colour, what colour would you be and why?

Where do you think is the best place for this colour to live in your body if you were to imagine you were made up of colour bands like a rainbow? How would it feel to wear your colour head to toe in clothing? What properties might it have do you think? Take it in turns to answer these same questions so everyone in the group has shared with everyone else.

16. What things do you take for granted in your life?

There are simple things that we take for granted in our lives every day, for example running water. What changes can we make to our behaviours in order to respect these privileges more? How can we value things better in our lives? What habits could we integrate in our lives to remind ourselves to feel gratitude? Take it in turns to answer these same questions so everyone in the group has shared with everyone else.

17. If you had to live on a desert island for the rest of your life on your own, what message would you put in a bottle for your loved ones to find?

Take it in turns to answer this same question so everyone in the group has shared with everyone else.

18. What is the main driving force in your life? Or to put it another way, what makes you move forward in your life? What motivates you most?

Drive is a force that makes you go forward. It's probably why we call driving a car driving (because mainly we use the vehicle to go forward and reach places). So how do you make sure you reach places? Take it in turns to answer this same question so everyone in the group has shared with everyone else.

19. What do YOU think intuition is? Where does it come from? How does it work? What do we use it for? Can everyone use it?

We hear this term more frequently nowadays, so enjoy discussing this one! Take it in turns to answer these same questions so everyone in the group has shared with everyone else.

20. What are the top 5 things that make you FEEL GOOD? How can you integrate more of these things into your life?

Take it in turns to answer this same question so everyone in the group has shared with everyone else.

21. If you were a Fairy or a Pixie what would your name be and where would you live? What would be your magical skill, unique to you in fairy land?

Take it in turns to answer these same questions so everyone in the group has shared with everyone else. Don't let dads or big brothers get away without answering this one!

22. What does forgiveness mean to you?

Ask this question first and take turns to share your answer with everyone. Then go on to dissect the subject more using the following exploratory questions: Who have you forgiven in your life? What is the difference between forgiveness and acceptance? When we forgive do we judge first - is this correct behaviour? How may we learn to accept without judgement? On a scale of 1-10 how hard to you think that would be to do?

23. If you could re-experience one moment of your life so far what would it be and why?

Take it in turns to answer this same question so everyone in the group has shared with everyone else.

24. What is it really like to be in someone else's shoes?

Pick a person who you have had an interaction with today - maybe they stood out to you for some reason, maybe you literally collided, maybe you helped them in some way or maybe they did something to annoy you. Now pretend you are living inside them and describe their world using your own voice. Take it in turns to answer this same question so everyone in the group has shared with everyone else and experienced being in 'someone else's shoes'.

25. If you HAD to give 1 million pounds away who would you give it to and why?

Take it in turns to answer this same question so everyone in the group has shared with everyone else.

26. 'Tomorrow is not Yesterday.' What does this statement mean to you? What are you going to do differently tomorrow compared to your yesterday?

Take it in turns to answer these same questions so everyone in the group has shared with everyone else.

27. If you were to believe we all have had past lives, which 3 past lives do you instinctively think or feel you have lived before? Talk about your reasons for choosing these three past lives?

Take it in turns to answer these same questions so everyone in the group has shared with everyone else.

28. If you could be any animal what would you be and why?

Take it in turns to answer this same question so everyone in the group has shared with everyone else.

29. What are your biggest fears in life?

They say fear is temporary but regrets last a lifetime so what do you fear most? How can you build the courage to conquer that fear, and reach your dreams? Take it in turns to answer these same questions so everyone in the group has shared with everyone else.

30. What is the funniest thing that's ever happened to you?

Can you remember laughing so much that your stomach ached? Why is laughing so good for us do you think? Take it in turns to answer these same questions so everyone in the group has shared with everyone else and if you're intrigued why laughter feels so good, read Chapter 4!

31. If you could grow a tree in the garden that grew any food on it, what type of tree would you grow?

For example, I'd like to grow a croissant tree! What would be the pros and cons of this tree? How would it need to be looked after? What animals would be attracted to the tree? How could you protect it from predators? How would it get pollinated to make more trees like it? My croissant tree would definitely need protection against hungry children and I think it would produce new trees by dropping its crumbs! Take it in turns to answer these same questions so everyone in the group has shared with everyone else.

32. What have you done today that is kind?

When you look back on your day, how could you have increased the level of kindness in your day? Take it in turns to answer these same questions so everyone in the group has shared with everyone else.

33. What do you understand by the term authenticity?

Give examples of when you think you are being authentic and how it feels? In what area of your life could you be more authentic? Take it in turns to answer these same questions so everyone in the group has shared with everyone else.

34. Share your Elevator Pitch.

This one will need some prep time, so I suggest you either ask the question at the start of the meal or gathering, let people reflect and think about what they might say, maybe giving people a sheet of paper to help plan their pitch and then share it at the end of the meal or over pudding! Please see the notes in the chapter '52 Helpful Prompts' No.34 for clarification on what this is! Take it in turns to share your pitch so everyone in the group has shared with everyone else.

35. What would your Avatar look like?

Using anyone you know, celebrity or film characters, and choose whose hair, face, body, personality, dress sense and talent you would have in order to create your perfect Avatar? Or you may like to make your Avatar up entirely from your imagination. Take it in turns to answer this same question so everyone in the group has shared their Avatar with everyone else.

36. Describe your future husband or wife!

Use this question as an opportunity to tune into your intuition and imagination and predict what your future spouse or life partner will be like. Describe their appearance, what job they may do and what their personality is like. If you are already married, then use this question as an opportunity to predict what another person's future spouse may be like in the group. Take it in turns to answer this same question so everyone in the group has shared with everyone else.

37. If you could choose to make your life decisions by one part of you, which part would it be? Your mind, your heart, or your soul? Why?

Take it in turns to answer this same question so everyone in the group has shared with everyone else.

38. If you were asked to play a leading role in a film which part would you choose?

Some examples might be The King or Queen, The Damsel, The Hero, The Warrior, The Magician, or The Lover. Why would you choose this role? What does your answer tell you about how you live your life right now? Take it in turns to answer this same question so everyone in the group has shared with everyone else.

39. If you were given 1 million pounds and it had to last a lifetime how would you make that million grow?

Note, that if you live until 100 years of age, 1 million pounds would equate to £27 a day! Take it in turns to answer this same question so everyone in the group has shared with everyone else.

40. Give 5 reasons why you love the person next to you!

Take it in turns to answer this same question so everyone in the group has shared their love with everyone else.

41.What do you need in order to reach your dream and make it a reality?

You can share what your dream is or not, your choice; but it's important to share what you think and feel you need (these could be practical things, emotional support, knowledge or a mixture of them all). What steps would you need to take in order to reach the goal you really want in life? Take it in turns to answer this same question so everyone in the group has shared their dream and plans with everyone else.

42.What is the ESSENCE of you?

Share this, and then also share what you feel is the essence of every other person in the group too. Take it in turns to answer the same question so everyone in the group has shared with everyone else.

43.What was the most embarrassing thing that you've ever done and why?

OK, so everyone has got something to share here! It just depends how honest you're going to be! We've had some hysterical stories come out when we've played this game - it's a real eye opener! Make sure you take it in turns to answer this same question so everyone in the group has shared with everyone else - nobody gets out of this one!

44.What do you think an Aura is?

When people say, 'that person has a good energy about them' or 'that person lights up a room when they walk in', what do you think they are talking about? If you could see it, what colour is the person's aura next to you do you think? (use your intuition to make a guess). Take it in turns to answer this same question so everyone in the group has shared with everyone else. If you are intrigued to know more about auras and energy management enjoy reading Chapter 10, you could even ask members of the group to read sections out loud for all to hear and then discuss the topic in more depth, sharing you own experiences.

45. If you caught a Genie in a bottle, which three wishes would you ask for and why?

Be careful here...there are always consequences! Take it in turns to answer this same question so everyone in the group has shared with everyone else.

46. What is the biggest or most significant thing that you have learnt in the last ten years?

Please adjust according to age and take it in turns to answer this same question so everyone in the group has shared their learning with everyone else.

47. If you could invent a magical potion, which ingredients would it contain and what properties would it have?

Take it in turns to answer this same question so everyone in the group has shared with everyone else.

48. Why try to fit in, when you were born to stand out? What makes you stand out from the crowd? What makes the person next to you stand out from the crowd?

Take it in turns to answer these same questions so everyone in the group has shared with everyone else.

49. Where do you think we all go when we die?

Take it in turns to answer this same question so everyone in the group has shared with everyone else. Please be accepting of differing views and encourage open discussion as great learning can be gained by listening to alternative views on religion and spiritual beliefs.

50. If you could paint your 'Graffiti Story' what would it be?

Describe the scene, the characters, the composition, the colours, the meanings, the overall ethos. Or, literally draw a picture for the group to see! Graffiti art is a conduit for expressing many topics in a public arena so you can use this question to express yourself and your life to the group! Members is the group can try and second guess what you are drawing as you complete the picture (a bit like in the familiar game Pictionary). Take it in turns to answer this same question so everyone in the group has shared with everyone else.

You may like to take more time over this question and use it as an opportunity to create some group art. You could either produce one large graffiti story painting, or individual ones that make up a tiled abstract collaboration. See Q50. In the 52 Helpful Prompts Chapter for further group activity ideas.

51. If you could change one thing about the world what would it be and why?

Take it in turns to answer this same question so everyone in the group has shared with everyone else.

52. Imagine for a moment your life has ended and you are able to see and hear your Eulogy being read out by one of your friends or family at your own funeral. What would you like that Eulogy to say? How can you align your life now in order to make that Eulogy possible in the future? What changes will you need to make in your present life in order to make it come true?

Take it in turns to answer this same question so everyone in the group has shared with everyone else and set the scene for a life that you all want to have lived! This is an important question which could bear relevance for many years to come! Because remember, we can create our reality with our intention!

My hope is that these 52 questions, however you approached working through them, have got your mind, spirit and soul thinking and feeling. That you have had many personal realisations and you have experienced revelations about the people in your friendship groups, family or people you work with. It may even open up a new window in your mind's eye...

I would also love to hear your stories, so if you would like to share some of the experiences you have shared with your family and friends when using these questions at gatherings, please do share a tweet using **#gatheringinsights**

52 Helpful Prompts

The sections in bold in this chapter can help you to adapt and re-phrase the questions if you need to explain them to younger children. The sections in italics are useful notes that will give extra 'Tid Bits' behind the intention of the question being asked. I have also included some useful recommendations for books, quotes and concepts that may be of interest to you in the bibliography section at the back of the book.

It's so important as parents to try and see a child's world through their eyes. This means even sometimes physically getting down to speak with them eye to eye, meeting them on their level (and that doesn't mean it's inferior - often children have the most honest and insightful things to share). As adults we can learn so much from their perception of the world because they look at things with fresh inquisitive minds, often free of fear or pre-conceived ideas. My hope is that you can find ways of using the 52 questions set out in this book as a conduit for communication and exploration with your child. It has the potential to bring you closer together, to see your child with fresh eyes and to increase the bond between family members as well as friends.

1. **Ask your child 'What one thing do you like most about ..... (another person in the group) and wish you could have yourself?' You could go on to then ask 'Why is that?'. Ask them to choose something they like about every single person in the group.**

   Note: This was one of the first questions I asked my family when I started experimenting with the idea of this book. We still have a great time sharing what attributes we would like to have from each other from time to time, as often it changes. What became evident very quickly was the appreciation and love we felt for each other. You could literally see people's faces light up when you said you loved an aspect of their personality. This exercise grows love, respect and self-esteem...such a great one to do time and time again. Enjoy!

2. **Ask a child to imagine they are King or Queen in charge of a castle and they have to make up 5 rules for their soldiers and villagers to live by!**

   Note: This can be really fun because no doubt you will hear children replay parts of films they have watched where Kings and Queens have ruled lands and had particular rules that they thought were good ones and bad ones.

   This question can give you a real insight into a child's developing principles that they will later learn to live their lives by. It's an excellent chance to ask them why they have chosen particular rules, what the consequences might be, what different types of people might think about the rules i.e. are they fair for everyone or not?

   You could also ask them to think about the rules that are imposed on them at pre-school or school and discuss which ones they think work well and which ones don't. Encourage them to discuss what their friends think about the school rules and how they would then compile their own list of school rules.

   If you are brave enough you could also ask them what they think about the rules at home (!) ask them how they feel being on the receiving end of these rules; what they would do differently and why. No doubt they will come up with some interesting alternatives!

3. Maybe your child has a favourite toy that they chose in a shop? You could remind them of the time when they first saw the toy, maybe even saved up their pocket money in order to afford it and then the feeling of exhilaration when they bought the toy and brought it home. Then discuss with them how over time their interest in the toy maybe changed...because other new toys came along. Ask them how that first toy now feels...explain that being 'in love' might be like the feeling of exhilaration they first had. But the decision to 'love' is when you still look after the toy and care for it even though there may be other newer toys since.

Note: This is a great opportunity to discuss the idea of responsibility and loving kindness and hear what they think about love through their own innocent eyes. Often children will form their own idea of love through their role models (often parents) and also how they themselves have been treated by others. So this exercise will give you an intimate insight into their internal world; their feelings about how they've been treated by others in the past, and how this has influenced their own communication style and the behaviours you may witness them using.

4. This is fun! I think most children will get this! 'If you could be any type of food what would you like to be?' 'What colour food and texture and shape would you like to be?'

Note: Make sure you ask why they have chosen the food they want to be as this can really get them to delve further into their imaginations and get more in touch with the 5 senses of sight, sound, touch, taste and smell. You could even take this question a little further with children and ask them how they think it is to be a carrot for example. You may get some very interesting answers and it may help you to understand their eating habits and reasons for preferences, something that often eludes us parents when preparing meals!

5. **Ask the child to think back to a time when they were learning something new; it could even be when they learnt to walk, ride a bike, write or get dressed, or something they learnt at school or a sport activity. Encourage them to share how it felt when they couldn't do the action, and how they changed their behaviour in order to achieve the goal. Ask 'What did you do differently when you started to be able to ride your bike?' Then you may ask questions such as 'When you started to be able to balance on your bike how did it feel?' 'What do you think you did differently from the time before when you fell off?' 'What will you do from now on, knowing you are able to ride?' 'How will you move differently to ensure you become the best bike rider ever?'**

Note: Professional sports coaches use a technique where they ask their students to go inside their body and ask:

No.1 What do I need to do next time in order to feel better at doing this?

No. 2 Where on a scale of 1-10 was I in terms of fluidity or strength or power (depending on the sport action goal)

No. 3 Where in my body do I need to make this change?

Then, they will visualise the change happening and start to feel the reaction they will have, once completing the improved action. This is a powerful skill as it encourages neural pathways (synapses) in the brain to grown in response to intention and then the physical ability is more likely to happen when performed in real time. Please refer to the bibliography for further reading on 'Coaching for Performance'.

6. **I think this question is already geared to a child! It's fun for adults to answer it too as we're all still children inside....or at least we should try and be!**

   Note: My son aged 15, at 6ft 2 inches tall, amused us all when we went out for dinner one night and I plucked this question from my growing list. We had never seen him more engaged with a conversation about anything! In fact we couldn't stop him getting into quite a heated discussion with my daughter about the pros and cons of certain superheroes and their weapons and super powers! It was so good to see the imagination and enthusiasm still there in a person who is normally an introverted and reluctant teen. Sometimes imagination just needs a little prod!

7. **You may like to take this opportunity to research 'Mother Nature' on the internet and find different definitions and theories as to what 'she' is. Help explain the different concepts you find, maybe that Mother Nature is the all-encompassing energy that nourishes and protects the planet or is literally the 'Soul' of our planet. You could look at some clips of video showing the destruction we humans cause and ask your child 'How do you think Mother Nature feels, what can we do to help her do you think?'**

   Note: My children learn about environmental awareness at their school but it's always good to explain the impact we as Individuals have on our planet from the home environment, explaining how we all have a responsibility to contribute to helping it to heal.

   Every small action can go towards making a difference to the whole of our planet. See the bibliography for some useful references and videos you can watch together.

8. **Children can use any statement in this exercise so encourage them to say something with 'I think' that is relevant to their world such as 'I think elephants are huge' and then 'I feel sad when baby elephants loose their Mummy'.**

Hopefully this way they will be able to sense where the statement comes from in their body - potentially two different places. Feeling statements tend to come from the heart, and thinking statements tend to come from our minds or head. These are two equally valid ways of interpreting data and making decisions but we don't always value the different qualities they bring. Children are likely to be better at differentiating between the heart and the mind compared to adults, as we tend to automatically assume all statements come from our mind!

If you would like to explore the relationship between the decision making parts of ourselves further you can try this exercise designed by Kinesiologist, Claire Kedward: Hold an imaginary 'Dinner Party' with your heart, mind, body and soul all sat at the table. Ask a question and listen to what each says in reply (they will all have a different perspective). You may even notice that mind doesn't listen to heart, or soul is not in agreement with body! You will soon notice they all have very different ideas! Ideally we would all listen to the four parts of our selves equally and consult on them to make decisions in our lives, but you may find one or two parts are in control more than the others. It is common for the mind to 'think' it's in control for example! You may like to help heart, mind, body and soul to communicate better by clarifying their different roles so they are each clear about what they are respectively responsible for. Then each will start to feel more valued.

If you are interested in learning more about the relationship between thinking and feeling, I can provide 1:1 MBTI coaching to help you understand your own personality preferences which in turn can help you become more effective in communicating with different people. Visit www.bristolreiki-healingarts.co.uk for more details and reference the bibliography at the end of this book.

9. **Simples! most children love music and sound so I don't think you'll have a problem asking this question! Have some fun playing examples of different music and asking how the different sounds make them feel...we often take turns on long car journeys to choose our favourite songs...it can be an interesting experience!**

Note: Did you know that sound can heal? Music, or sound is really just another type of energy. Just as colour is a frequency of light, music is a frequency of sound. Both colour and sound can help balance our own energetic system (or aura). Each of us has a certain energetic frequency, therefore we will be attracted to sounds that complement our energetic makeup. So, if you pay attention to the sounds people choose to listen to, it can tell you a great deal about the mood or 'energetic space' they are in that day.

Drumming is an example where people can come together and produce sound collaboratively. The collective beat is greater than the individual beat, so energies are raised and cleared as a result. Have you ever danced around a fire listening to drums? It's a wonderfully grounding experience. So next time you feel you need to clear some stuck emotions or thoughts, get out your favourite tunes and dance! Sing along and you will open your throat chakra, shake down the vibes around your body and you will clear your whole aura and ground your energy!

Sound healing is another way you can use the vibration of sound to clear stagnant energy in the body. This technique uses instruments such as drums, bells, gongs and singing bowls to balance and clear our energetic body. You typically lie on the ground on mats with blankets and pillows and allow the vibrations of sounds to wash over you. This technique is delivered by trained therapists and can induce meditative states to help calm the mind and body. You may like to experience sound healing in your local area - if you are based in the South West of England I can highly recommend Celia Beeson and her events on www.soundscape.org.uk.

10. Not many people really understand what the 'Soul' is, so your answer and interpretation will be personal to you; but in order to help here, simply ask a child 'Your Soul is what would be left if you didn't have your body'. You may like to talk about angels, or ghosts or spirits as you see fit, (within the boundaries of your religious or spiritual beliefs), or maybe you feel open enough to talk freely about all types of belief. This would be particularly useful for a child so they can make up their own mind, unhindered by preconceptions. The main intention here is for your child to think about what feeds that invisible but very poignant part of them. You may like to ask what things they like doing that fills them up inside, like imagining an empty glass being filled with a lovely juice! The glass is the body, but what and where is the juice?

Note: Often as adults we talk about our 'Soul' being nourished by certain activities that are congruent with our character or the type of person we are. Being an artist, I can identify fully with Pablo Picasso's quote "Art washes away from the Soul the dust of every day life". But for some this would not relate. For some of you, walking in nature, cooking, or climbing a mountain may nourish your Soul. The point is, identifying that it needs to be done is the first important step. Your Soul needs feeding, and you need to ascertain what types of 'food' will help keep it nourished!

11. This question should go down well when you describe travelling in a rocket to a planet in the sky to start up a new home! Depending on the age of the child you can perhaps show some images of Mars on the internet and explain how in the future scientists may be able to change the habitat of Mars so it is habitable, like earth.

Note: You may like to explain to the child and share in the group the work that Elon Musk is doing with the project SpaceX. See the bibliography for useful resources.

12. You can have some fun with children when asking this question, if you dare! Try turning it around - ask your child to take the role of parenting you and see if they can come up with some important life rules for you to live by! You'll probably get some interesting answers and certainly a real insight into how they perceive you and how you live your life!

Note: You may like to use this as a separate opportunity to allow them to draw up some house rules and parenting rules and swop roles for the day... I dare you!

13. This too is a fun question. You may need to encourage their imagination as young children may not yet have travelled abroad to experience other countries or cultures as much as you have. However, remember how fertile a child's imagination is, so encourage them to include fantasy worlds too!
They may like to visit Narnia! I know I would like to have a drink in the 'Cantina Bar' on the planet of 'Tatooine' in 'Star Wars' and also fly through the 'Avatar' jungle on the back of 'Puff The Magic Dragon'!

Note: Always keep the child in you alive! Albert Einstein said "Imagination is everything, it is the preview of life's attractions". Quantum Physics now confirms that the mind is a powerful tool that can be used to imagine what we desire - setting emotive intention to literally create the life we want to live. What we imagine and believe to be true can actually manifest in front of us!

Jim Carrey has given some inspiring speeches related to this topic. I love his quote 'let your heart be playful'. I have included the search title for Jim Carrey's speech in the bibliography at the end of this book so you can enjoy the enthusiasm and motivational message he sends out to his anticipating audience.

14. With this one, maybe you can ask 'When you are playing in the garden or woods or at the park, do you ever feel that you are not alone (although Mum or Dad may be close by) and there is a feeling that something else is with you or next to you, keeping you company?' OR 'when you are by the huge ocean do you feel alone or do you feel there is something larger with you that you are part of?' 'If this is true what do you think it is?'

Note: This question's aim is to get people to sense outside of themselves and observe their connection to their environment, to nature, to the world, to others and maybe to the invisible realm of energy. Its designed to get us thinking about how we are one, we are all made of the same atoms and elements and so there is connection with everything around us whether it is a man made object or a living thing in nature.

Children are typically more receptive to these sensations because they are open to using all their senses including their sixth sense! The answers you get from children can be really interesting so do explore and be open minded with them.

You may need to be sensitive to the fact that some children may feel a little scared by the thought that 'someone may be watching over them', so please reassure them and encourage an open dialogue about the possibilities of angels or spirit guides who look after us. Or you may prefer to say how the stars at night watch over us and ask how they think we are connected to the universe, solar system, sun and moon.

15. This is another easy one for children to relate to...I remember discussing my favourite colour with my friends as a child. Discuss the different friends they have and how their 'energy' is different. You could even ask whether your child sees colours around people (often children are capable of seeing auras around the body) and they are also more open to sensing things we adults can't see. This can be a very revealing question!

Note: Did you know we are all drawn to colours for a reason? The body is made up of 7 energy centres called chakras and they maintain and balance our overall health, distributing energy to the organs in the body, making sure we are working at an optimum level.

By wearing colours and eating coloured foods and even placing coloured crystals on the chakra points of our body, we can help to re-balance them. Sometimes the stresses and strains of modern day life can mean that the chakras become out of balance. If there is a colour you are often drawn to wearing maybe there is a reason? Maybe you need more of this colour or maybe it feels congruent with your own aura (personal energy field).

The chakras are in a sequence of colours like a rainbow, the same light frequencies you get when light is split by a prism. Colour is a wonderful commodity to use in our daily lives to help heal the dis-ease of every day life. If you are interested in learning more about the chakra system visit www.bristolreiki-healingarts.co.uk and you can book a chakra balancing treatment. Also refer to the bibliography for resources about colour therapy and the chakras.

16. **This is a good opportunity for your gathering to watch a film about the poverty around the world or even in your own city. You could also share experiences you've had seeing people in poverty and how it made you feel.**

Note: It's always good to remind ourselves how lucky we are and spread gratitude as there are always people coping in life with much less. You can ask your child after watching some video footage about their views and discuss how other communities survive. Talk about which simple things we tend to take for granted in our homes and then how as families we can learn to be more efficient with the resources we are so lucky to have.

Also discuss how you express gratitude more often, maybe start a new habit in the family which encompasses this idea - like a family gratitude book, for example. Even something as simple as going around the table at mealtimes and saying 3 things each person feels grateful for receiving during the day can make a real difference to the way we perceive our world.

Personally, I like to give gratitude for the things I have experienced from my day before I go to sleep at night and I also like to give thanks for the day ahead each morning. This links in nicely with setting an intention for the day. Please refer to the bibliography for further resources on the topic of gratitude.

17. This is a question that requires quite a bit of thought, so you may like to set the scene at the start of your gathering and let the ideas percolate! A child may respond well to the analogy of Robinson Crusoe (if they are familiar with the classic story) and how he was stranded on a desert island. They may also like the idea of pirate ships and how the bottle they set to sail (with its message inside) may end up being found by the 'Pirates of the Caribbean' boat! Jack Sparrow could himself sail it back to England and deliver it to their loved ones to read! Have some fun and construct a story using these kinds of themes for the child's message in a bottle!

Note: The intention behind this question is to encourage you to literally encapsulate the wisdom you have gained in your life so far, in a single message for your loved ones. Although a little morbid I always appreciated the 'funeral idea' from Steven Covey in his book 'The Seven Habits of Highly Effective People'.

Here he suggests that we all project forward and imagine a scene at our own funeral where friends and family gather to celebrate (hopefully!) our lives. He asks you to write down what you would hope a relative or friend would read out to the congregation in memory of your life.

This exercise consolidates and focuses the mind on what was really poignant and essential in your life. It helps you to re-focus your path in current reality and adapt and change your course if needs be. A powerful tool for setting intention and realigning what you desire for your life going forward and how to set it in motion. Please refer to the bibliography for details about Steven Covey's book.

18. One of the first driving forces for a baby is food...crying is an instinctive reaction in order to survive. But I wonder if a child can identify with the driving force behind learning to walk? Why do young toddlers get up from falling time and time again when they first learn to walk? Or, learning to ride a bike...what is behind that driving force? Using these as examples to ask a child 'What was it that made you keep trying and trying when you were learning to ride your bike? I saw you struggle and get frustrated, sometimes falling off and feeling like giving up, but what was it that kept you going?'. The answers they give can be very insightful for both their personal development and your view of them.

Note: Maslow's Hierarchy of Needs shows us how we are all programmed to satisfy the first 3 basic needs (food & water, shelter, and love). Until these basic needs are met, the theory explains how it is impossible to achieve the higher levels of satisfaction and ultimately enlightenment. It seems these basic needs are driven by an instinct, so what are our other desires driven by, such as learning to play an instrument or master a sport? Where in our bodies does this drive live? Learning what motivates a person can give a real insight into their personality and the way they live and order their life...after all, it's what makes us all tick!

You may like to take the subject of motivation a little further in your gathering and explore what motivates each person by asking them to describe how they felt when they remember a time when they were really motivated and enthused in an activity. One person can list the descriptive words they use while they talk and then repeat the exercise for a time when the other person felt bored and un-inspired to take action. Take it in turns to go around the room and capture each person's responses for how they felt when they were enthused and how they felt when they were bored. Once each person has their list, you can take it in turns to prioritise the words and come up with each person's top 3 motivators and de-motivators. These insights will then help parents, friends and colleges understand how to get the best out of the other people in the group in future projects or activities.

19. Children are often much more intuitive than us adults because they do not have the need as yet to rationalise thoughts. They just feel or trust their instincts. It may be challenging to explain this to a child as they will likely see it as a normal practice. You may be able to help clarify the meaning by asking 'When you see a snail on the ground and you imagine stamping on it or picking it up and placing it carefully out of harm's way, which do you believe is the right thing to do?' Hopefully they will answer saying the latter...if you ask them 'How do you know that is the right thing to do?' they may say because Mummy told me so, but they may also say 'it just is'. This is an example where we just 'know' instinctively what is right and what is wrong. If we were to choose the wrong action we know we would get a horrible feeling inside, an awkwardness, a feeling that we are not being authentic to our true nature as a human being. Some children are so in tune with their intuition, they just know when something is wrong, they can't put it into words, but they just have a sense of something. Use this time to discuss those moments...it's really eye opening and interesting to watch their reactions to your questions.

Note: I like to feel that fundamentally we would all choose the right thing to do, it is only through conditioning in our environment and through experience that that choice may become distorted. We all surely start from a place of love, respect and caring? The definition of intuition goes something like this: "Intuition is the ability to acquire knowledge without proof, evidence, or conscious reasoning, or without understanding how the knowledge was acquired....The word intuition comes from the Latin verb intueri translated as "consider" or from the late middle English word intuit, "to contemplate". I wonder where intuition is generated in our bodies? Is it in our 'gut' hence the expression 'I feel it in my gut' or does it come from our Soul?

20. Simply ask a child 'What are your 5 favourite things that make you feel really good?' Once they have answered, say 'how can you get more of these into your life'? Children should find this quite easy to answer as they don't have the social filters and constraints compared to adults.

Note: They are much more likely to be honest about what they want in life, as when they are babies they are programmed to demand what they need as a matter of survival and this continues into toddlerhood (which is why we find the obstinate tantrums challenging!). Actually they are just saying what THEY want. We then try as adults to teach them to understand life is not just about what THEY want but they need to consider others too. This, however, is where suppression and constraint come into the mix! A balance obviously needs to be learnt in order to become an effective and emotionally intelligent adult. For some this is less well learned than for others as we find out later on in life! Remember it's not selfish to require or need things.

One of the most important things I learnt in my Reiki training was to nourish, love and look after yourself first and then the well of love you create for yourself can overflow like a fountain to others. During an airplane flight they always say 'put on your oxygen mask first and then help your child'. This seems odd at first, but you would be no help whatsoever to your children unless you secure your lifeline first in order to be there for them. This is the same principle. It is crucial to identify what things you need most in life. That way you can grow to your full potential and then help others to flourish. So, each day I like to ask myself 'what do I need today in order to feel good?' Every day is different, but there are often common themes. Start today - ask yourself this question and see how your holistic balance improves.

21.I don't think I need to help you with this one...but I can't wait to hear what Dad's reply will be!

Note: Although you may think 'What on earth is the value in asking this question in a mixed age group?', there is huge value. Firstly, it engages the younger audience and gives you as an adult an insight into the world of a child, and the potential of your own imagination. You can still learn a great deal about a person's personality preferences and their drive and motivations from fun questions like this. In fact, because it engages the child in us all, we are more likely to get in touch with our true nature and then that's when self-awareness arises.

22.The simplest way to demonstrate forgiveness to your child can be using the example of sharing toys. We know how often children fight over the same toy, but we teach them to share. Maybe you can remind your child of a time they fought over a toy with a friend or sibling and then 'forgave' the other child afterwards. It's interesting to delve into their answer a little bit too...asking what it felt like during and after.

Note: One of my favourite spiritual teachers is Caroline Myss and she suggests that in fact when we forgive it actually means we have already therefore judged the person in the first place. I think this is true. Of course forgiveness is still better than nothing, but I do think how wonderful it would be if we could all learn to accept those tough things that happen to us without judgement.

What would YOU need in order to accept all that has happened to you in your life? What support do you feel you need in order to forgive more readily? These are deep questions, but ones worth asking. We all hold onto experiences from the past like echoes. Some still serve us, but others do not, so it is good practice to give yourself a spring clean every now and again and resolve any unfinished business. Writing letters to the people we need to forgive can help in this process. You don't necessarily need to send them, the simple practise of bringing the feelings out on to paper can heal.

23. Ask a child 'What has been the best time in your life so far? It could be something today, yesterday, last week or last year or longer ago. Tell me the first thing that comes into your mind. Why was it the best thing ever?

Note: Appreciate that children have a different perception of time to us adults. Young children live in the present moment, which is wonderful and ironically what us adults try to get back to all the time! Therefore, your child may only remember what they did yesterday or even a few hours ago. It doesn't matter...as this question can be applied to any timeframe and any answers will hold gems of insight. When adults reply to this question it's a good idea to respond with the first thing that comes to mind. If you deliberate for too long that means you are intellectualising the answer. Go with your gut! Use that instinctive part of you and see what comes out! Remember you will also answer different things on different days.

24. You may like to use the phrase 'Put yourself in the other person's shoes' - a well known saying, and a wise one at that, it's good to explain this to your child as it will help grow emotional intelligence. Perhaps you can literally ask them to go and get a family member's shoes, putting them on and pretending to be that other person for a moment and then ask them to explain how it feels to be that person. Encourage them to imagine they go invisible and leave their own body and dissolve inside the other person's body; so taking on the shape of the body, and all the feelings and thoughts and emotions of that person. This can be really fun and revealing!

Note: This question can be a great way to develop your child's understanding that the world does not just revolve around them. Other people have feelings and experiences too and you can encourage them to practise this on other occasions. It will increase their ability to empathise and ultimately increase emotional intelligence.

25. Depending on the age of the child, they may struggle to understand the value of 1 million pounds as after all £10 is a great deal of money to a 5 year old! Either way, use an appropriate amount of money based on the age of the child so they feel it is a significant amount of money that they HAVE to give away (they can't keep for themselves). Hopefully they will think long and hard before answering and you will I'm sure get some interesting responses.

Note: This question is insightful because it can indicate the type of principles and values a person may have and also how they approach problem solving. Some people will automatically assume that giving a large sum of money away to the poor or needy is the best solution reaping the greatest benefit, and that may be true for the individual. But other people who think more strategically, may decide that greater change for good could be achieved by giving the same lump sum of money to a person who is in a position of power or influence. Because that money can go to a cause, grow and be given to larger communities for a greater good.

You can use this discussion to brainstorm ideas and encourage members of the group to think laterally. It's not always the most obvious of solutions that will make the most significant difference.

Also consider whether the outcome needs to be about making more money available to people, or can it be used to produce something else that will make a difference? Instead of thinking about profit as a monetary gain, maybe see the word profit in a different light...how can you make something in favour of fitness...a fitter planet or society? Pro-fit instead of Profit. We use the word profit so readily in the economy, maybe it's time to transform this word into something more value driven?

26. The concept of time is a tricky one for young children, but you may like to try reminding a child what they did yesterday, where they went...talk to them about what they might be doing tomorrow, maybe school or a swimming lesson or visiting the park? Then ask them 'What will you do differently at the park (or wherever) tomorrow, compared to what you did at the zoo?'. Try and help them to identify the practical things they will do differently and the different behaviours they will exhibit.

Note: This will encourage children to think about differences in time and also learning from the past and then applying that learning to the future. As adults, it's one of the most important things we can do in order to transform ourselves. If we don't reflect on previous experiences and then apply the learning the next time, we can become stagnant. Something I learnt in my previous role as a people development consultant was to encourage people to write a reflection note whenever they experienced or did something new.

It can be as simple as asking:

1. What was the new thing I did?

2. What went well about it?

3. What didn't go so well and why?

4. What will I do differently next time?

5. What could the impact be if I chose to do it differently?

You may like to try this the next time you do something different in your life, it could be a project at work, a new sport or hobby or a simple task at home. You'll be surprised how valuable the reflection can be.

27. Children, as we know, are much more open to ideas and concepts than we are. This is because they come into our world with open eyes and no preconception about how the world should be. Society, the way we are brought up by our families, and our early experiences growing up, create paradigms (lenses through which we see life). These paradigms are not necessarily accurate, but we think they are because we have become used to them. This question is a great opportunity to see how younger children and adults feel about the idea of past lives. You may be surprised by some of their answers. It's most helpful to offer a neutral opinion yourself while explaining the concept so you don't enforce your own views on them before they answer the question.

Note: Some people believe that our Soul or Spirit never dies. Quantum physics after all does say that energy never disappears; it is only transformed into something different. Many people find relief in knowing their own Soul will in fact travel beyond the body it is currently housed in and will find a dwelling place in a new body or 'vehicle' for another lifetime.

Hypnotherapy can help people travel back into the subconscious where they are able to remember aspects of their previous lifetimes, and sometimes it is helpful to heal trauma from those previous lifetimes so we can be free of the same anchors in this present lifetime.

Some religions support the idea of past lives and some do not. So, it really is a question of what YOU believe and not a belief based on society's 'rules' or religious boundaries, but what you feel is right about your own Soul's existence. Please refer to the bibliography for further reading and resources.

28. Have some fun with this one...come on, you must have secretly always dreamed of being a particular animal... I'm sure your child has!

Note: Animals are often synonymous with mystical meanings suggesting that if you see a particular animal or manifest it during meditation, it can be representative of a certain stage or transition in your life. Shamanic practices teach that people have 'spirit animals' who can be called upon to assist in a person's development and path in life. I wonder what spirit animal you may have guiding you? Please refer to the bibliography for resources on this subject and a fun quiz to try (remember though, you are always the best judge, and need to use your intuition to determine your spirit animal accurately!).

29. Hopefully children don't hold too many regrets at their young stage in life but it's really useful to talk to them about fear and how as adults this so often holds us back. A child probably remembers times when they were too afraid to do something new. I remember at school standing on the top diving board for 30 minutes in my lunch hour trying to pluck up the courage to jump. Ask your child 'When was the last time you were too afraid to do something?' 'What would you do differently now if you were trying to do it for a second time?' We can learn so much from children so why not also ask them: 'What advice would you give adults who are trying to be less afraid of change or doing something new?' and see what they come up with!

Note: Please refer to the bibliography for more information on how to conquer your fears and some inspiring films to watch!

30. A simple question that any child will hopefully enjoy recollecting. I don't think you'll need much prompting with this one...there are bound to be lots of funny stories!

Note: I've pulled together some interesting ideas about why laughing is good for us in Chapter 4 of this book. I also suggest ways in which we can invite more laughter and fun into our lives.

31. Children can let their imaginations run wild with this one! I don't think they'll need much help here, apart from narrowing down their choice! I hope the adults have some fun with this too!

Note: Albert Einstein said "imagination is everything, it is the preview of life's coming attractions". Without imagination life would be a very mundane place, so it's important we feed our imaginations whenever and wherever we can! That way we can invite all kinds of possibilities into our lives!

32. Try asking 'If you fall, and you are picked up and hugged, what is that feeling you get from the other person who has comforted you?... It's kindness, caring, love and support. What can you remember you have done today that produced the same feeling for the other person?' 'How have you played with your toys? Your friends? Your pets?' 'Have you comforted anyone?'

Note: This is important as it helps the child to see that their world doesn't just revolve around them, that they have an impact on the world too and that other people and (even objects) have feelings.

Try and get them to share how they behave with the belongings they interact with in their inquisitive young lives. It may be recalling how they look after their pets; how they play with their toys; how they behave in the garden around the plants and insects they find; how they interact with friends and how they react when family members are upset.

Kindness is one of the most precious FREE things we can give people - I believe that single acts of loving kindness can actually help transform our world.

33. Try explaining this to a child by asking, 'if you were a superhero like superman and you ignored someone in danger and flew away, you would NOT be acting with authenticity because we all know superman saves people - that's what makes him special. So what action would you be doing if you were to be true to yourself like superman is when he saves people?' 'What makes you an authentic superhero?'

Note: This is a complex meaning for a child to grasp but by using the analogy of a superhero and making them understand that people expect a superhero to act in a certain way, but if they don't, they are not acting in congruence with their true nature; we can at least start to get them thinking about authenticity and the impact this has on ourselves and others around us.

34. This question is aimed at adults who need to present to a group or walk into a crowd and make an immediate impactful impression. Children can use this technique to 'sell' themselves to their friends or simply imagine they are being selected as a secret agent or squad of people with a special mission and they have to make sure to impress the selection panel so they are selected! You could use the analogy of some of the secret agent films they might have watched to get them into role. Alternatively, you can simply suggest 'If you only had 1 minute to say what you are like to a new friend, what words would you use to impress them and make sure they don't forget you?'

Note: An elevator pitch is a brief, persuasive speech that you use to spark interest in what you are about as a person; essentially what you have to offer. A good elevator pitch should last no longer than a short elevator ride of 20 to 30 seconds, hence the name. They should be interesting, memorable, and succinct. Please refer to the bibliography for resources about how to write your own elevator pitch.

35. This question will certainly ignite a child's imagination! Remember the film 'Avatar' by James Cameron? Well this is a chance to create your own Avatar! It's worth explaining to a child that in modern day life and in the tech industry, an Avatar is deemed as a 'personalised graphical illustration' that represents a computer user, or a character or alter ego that represents that user. An Avatar can be represented either in three-dimensional form (for example, in games or virtual worlds) or in two-dimensional form as an icon in Internet forums.

Note: An avatar (Sanskrit: avatāra), is a concept in Hinduism that means "descent" and refers to the material appearance or incarnation of a deity on earth. The relative verb "to alight, to make one's appearance" is sometimes used to refer to any guru or revered human being and may also be used to describe an incarnation of God. If you are interested to understand more about the term Avatar in relation to different religious belief systems, please refer to the bibliography for further information and resources.

This exercise can be extended to an art activity with children (and adults). Try drawing or using magazine cut outs to collage your ideal Avatar. If you are a family, you could all produce an Avatar (including the pets!) and frame it for the world to see! If you're feeling ultra creative you could even model your Avatars using plasticine, or air drying clay and paint them with acrylic paints to really bring them to life! Have fun... let your heart be playful!

36. Help a child to get in touch with their intuition and imagination by asking some preliminary questions like 'can you imagine 'name of person in group' being married to a person with red hair or blonde hair? Would they be tall or short? Funny or serious? etc. This will start them on a chain of thought, so they can manifest a whole identity and image of what they think the person they will be marrying one day will be like. If easier, you could ask people in the group to answer this question for each other instead.

Note: We often forget how powerful our primitive instincts are. Did you realise we can make a decision about a person and how much we are attracted to them in the first 3 seconds of meeting them?

Our unconscious mind is very powerful (like the hard drive of a computer) always working away in the background. Very often we make judgements about people based on primitive programming. It could be that we 'recognise' a pattern of behaviour or trait in a person that reminds us of our parents when we were very young and because our minds look for familiarity, we resonate with that person who is similar or shows similar behaviours. Or it could be that we are attracted to certain geometry in the way a person's facial components are arranged. Pheromones (which are personal hormones or secretions from the body) can be attractive or not attractive to us, even though we may think we find the image of a person pleasing.

So, who is to say we can't tap into our unconscious mind and actually be pretty accurate in predicting what type of person we may end up being life partners with! Or indeed be able to do this for another person - see into their future!

37. Start by asking a child where their mind (thinking) is held in their body; where their heart is held; and where their soul is held. This should be enlightening in itself! Ask them "When you have to make an important decision, for example 'should I let that other child play with my toy?' where do you think that decision came from?" 'Is it one place, two places or all three?' 'Which do you trust or like using more and why?'

Note: They say heart intelligence is much more powerful than mind intelligence...they say the soul is the connection to your creator (whoever you believe that to be), to divine light, to the spark within, to the cosmos, to everything, to 'Oneness'. What do you believe? Share your thoughts with the group if you would like to discuss this further.

Which place in your body do you make your decisions from? Does it depend on the decision? Should it depend on the decision? Is there one area you use more than the others? Is this something you would be best to change? How in touch are you with all the three areas? How would your decisions change if you used all 3? What order would you use them in? What could be the knock-on effect if you used all 3 in your life?

If you would like to explore the relationship between the decision making parts of ourselves further you can try this exercise designed by Kinesiologist, Claire Kedward: Hold an imaginary 'Dinner Party' with your heart, mind, body and soul all sat at the table. Ask a question and listen to what each says in reply (they will all have a different perspective). You may even notice that mind doesn't listen to heart, or soul is not in agreement with body! You will soon notice they all have very different ideas! Ideally we would all listen to the four parts of our selves equally and consult on them to make decisions in our lives, but you may find one or two parts are in control more than the others. It is common for the mind to 'think' it's in control for example! You may like to help heart, mind, body and soul to communicate better by clarifying their different roles so they are each clear about what they are respectively responsible for. Then each will start to feel more valued.

38. **Ask a child 'What is your favourite film?' Then ask them to replace the main characters with people in their family or friends. This will engage them with the question because they are using familiar people in the roles. Then they will be more likely to engage with the idea of themselves in a role and how they might feel playing it. You could also recollect times when they may have played parts in plays at school and compare how they felt in different roles.**

Note: This is a good way to develop a child's awareness of being in roles and the kind of behaviours that manifest out of different responsibilities. If you sit down and list the roles that you currently have in your life, you'll no doubt be surprised by how many you play! Each role has a different set of responsibilities and expectations from others. It just shows how adaptable human beings are!

This can in itself be a fun family or group exercise so you may like to sit together and list all the roles you play in your life. Once everyone has completed their list, exchange it with the person sat next to you and discuss how you both manage the different roles in your life using the questions below and then share a summary of your findings back to the group in turns.

1. Are their roles you'd like to change or even stop all together?

2. Are all your roles really necessary?

3. How much responsibility to do you take on versus giving others more duties or tasks?

4. What different proportions of time do your different roles take up in your life?

5. Is the time balance right when compared to the role's level of importance?

6. What things could you change in order to gain a better balance in your life roles?

39. This question requires a child to understand the value of money so it will help to explain how much it costs to run a home and put food on the table for example. You may like to share some of these expenses so they gain a more accurate picture of your household costs and also talk about how they can contribute when they are teenagers!

Note: Younger children may struggle to fully understand the concept but will benefit from hearing the discussion arising from this question. Older children who may have started to earn pocket money will be surprised at the cost of living no doubt!

Either way, we all think 1 million pounds is a huge amount of money (and it is). However, it's a sobering thought that this only equates to £27 a day if you lived for 100 years.

For some poor countries this would feed a small village of people in rice for a day or provide them with clean water, so making a significant improvement to their lives. In the rest of the world this amount of money would seem small.

This question can bring up some interesting opinions on what we 'need' and what we 'want' in life and what principles we hold in line with this. Each family will have its own 'perspective' of what is 'comfortable living' or not, so it's a useful discussion to bring up. Each person should be encouraged to search their values and share their perspective on the value of money. You may find you need to adjust some of your spending habits in line with the answers you hear!

40. **Love - such a big word in our lives but such a simple act. Children are born full of love. As adults we often become hardened to love because of painful experiences. Maybe we have been hurt or let down and then we are fearful of that happening again. Children will relate to the idea of 'Love' when they are reminded about their relationship with family (if they have been fortunate enough to be nourished in this way) and/or their favourite toys or pets, close friends or guardians, so encourage them to find this loving kindness and share what they love about the person next to them.**

Note: They say 'Love' is a choice, and an action. If we demonstrate loving kindness, 'Love' will grow from it. So, whoever is next to you, tell the child in this gathering that they have a choice to love them for who and what they are. It's simple. Sharing how you love them will bring out warmth and appreciation.

I believe that what we project onto other people is reflected back to us. So if you are feeling loved right now, that is no doubt because that is what you have given out. In actual fact, you are feeling your own love reflected back to you by the people you choose to love. The more love you project and send out, the more love you will receive!

We all like to give out love in similar ways to how we like to receive it, so if you enjoy being given lost of affection, hugs and holding hands then it is likely you will demonstrate this when you give love too someone. If you like receiving verbal compliments as a sign of love then it is likely you will give compliments to the ones you love. 'The Five Love Languages'. By Gary Chapman is a wonderful book that helps you to identify which love languages you respond to most readily and therefore how you are likely to express your love to others. It's a book that can be used to foster and nourish all the relationships in our lives. I highly recommend you reading this as it can transform the way you behave in an intimate relationship and help 'iron out' differences in the way we express love so promoting a more loving relationship in the future. See the bibliography for further details.

41. To simplify this question for a child, ask them 'What do you most want? It can be anything, how will you go about getting that thing?'. Allow a child to use their imagination to be or achieve ANYTHING they want to, it doesn't matter how crazy it may be!

Note: For example, if you want to be a fairy, how would you start? Where would you go, what would you do, what would you need to change about who you are right now? Would you have to grow wings? How would you do that? Think about the way it would happen...We all need dreams and goals in life - HOPE is what keeps us going. I

f you want to take this question another step further afterwards, how about drawing out on a large piece of paper your current reality for your dream (it's best to draw this at the bottom of the paper, so describe in your words where you are right now, and what the situation currently is) and then at the top of the paper write where you want to be (the desired outcome, so what it will look like when you have achieved your dream or goal). It's important to write the current reality in the present tense and then also write the desired outcome in the present tense (as if you have already attained it). Then you are sending the universe a message - that you have already acquired your dream. The space on the page in between the current reality and desired outcome is where you can then place some milestones (or points in time when you think you will have reached specific targets along the way). This will help you keep on track and stay motivated. If you so wish, each milestone can then be transferred to an action list on a separate page for you to work through. This is a great method for working out how you will achieve a desired outcome and the beauty is you can apply it to anything you wish for! It's also a really good tool to use in project management or strategic planning at work.

42. Have some fun with this one...ask a child 'What flavour ice cream would each person in the group be and why?' You could also use what fragrance, or what colour etc. *Note: It's important that the child is guided to express a representative 'essence'. This should bring out some humorous and insightful responses, particularly if they are asked to explain why Daddy is chocolate chip for example!*

43. This question is very entertaining and children will no doubt have some real revelations to share! It just depends how honest everyone is prepared to be! I wish I could share with you a story my teenage son told us that had us in stitches around the table! He would NEVER forgive me, so I can't. Enjoy this one!

   Note: To encourage children to build their confidence, I would suggest a couple of adults take their turn first as that way the children will feel more confident to be imaginative and the mood in the group may already have been lightened with laughter by the wild answers the adults divulge!

44. It is said that children are more sensitive to subtle energies and therefore more likely to see auras around people. So, it would be interesting to ask a child 'when you look at people, do you see any colours around them?' If the answer is 'yes', explore what the colours are like and ask the child what they think they represent.

   Note: You could use the analogy of a rainbow, explaining that light is refracted through rain drops which create the colours which make up a prism of light. Each colour in the rainbow resonates at a certain frequency (a bit like the different notes in music making up sound) and so people tend to have certain light frequencies around them depending on their mood, their interests and skills. Sometimes we get a sense that a person may have a dark cloud over them - I wonder if actually what we are sensing is their aura, and that maybe on that day in particular it is a darker colour than normal because they are carrying stress? People's auras are said to extend far beyond their physical body and they can have many layers to them. Please use the bibliography for further reading on this subject.

45. Every child likes the story of the Genie in the bottle and how when the bottle is rubbed the Genie appears and grants three wishes! So, there shouldn't be much difficulty engaging children with this question!

Note: Of course, the trick however is to realise that all decisions do have consequences, so how do you make sure you ask for the right wishes? Do you give your wishes away to anyone or could you grant someone a wish who could make a big difference in the world? Aim to explain how our actions or decisions in life always bear consequences, not necessarily good or bad, but consequences none the less.

46. This question is best asked according to the proportionate age of the person, so if for example a child is 10 years old, it would seem appropriate to ask 'What is the most important thing you have learnt in the last year?'. Please adjust the timescales accordingly so the question feels relevant to their memory span and the amount of experience they may have gained.

Note: Children learn at a rate much faster than adults (in general). Their brains are like sponges absorbing every detail they see and feel. This is partly why time travels much more slowly for them and instead why adults find time seems to speed up as we get older. Adult brains scan the environment for new data, but often because we fall into familiar patterns and territory (i.e. returning to the same holiday destination because we know we'll like it) our brains stop using energy to absorb and learn new things. This speeds everything up. Ever wondered why when you choose a new holiday destination the holiday seems longer, or at least it does for the first part until familiarity sets in! If we want to stretch time in our lives, we should all aim to do something new each day and feed our curious minds. That way we will extend our perception of time because we are busy taking in new information. If you would like to learn more about how time is distorted and how you may manipulate it in your own life, please refer to the bibliography for further reading.

47. This is a bit of fun, so children should enjoy using their imaginations to come up with some gruesome potions, no doubt with bat's eyes and lizard tongues in!

Note: The more serious side of this question could be about which magical properties the potion may give you...we all like the idea of being invisible or reading other peoples' minds, but would we really want these skills in reality? Could there be some down sides?

48. We all know that children seek to 'fit in' (in general) and as adults, some of us come to appreciate that it's actually really beneficial to 'own' one's diversity and stand out, so you can be recognised for the individual skills you can bring to the table.

Note: Encourage a child answering this question to think about how they are unique, and how that is a really positive attribute in life. You may like them to ask what makes the person next to them stand out first so they understand the concept, and then they may realise how it really is a benefit being 'different from everyone else'. Then they are more likely to feel confident in identifying what it is about them that makes them unique.

I know from my own experience as a Mother children tend to pick out differences in other children and can sometimes be cruel with their words in response. It amazes me how what I find is beautiful and unique (such as auburn hair) can be seen as a negative thing in a child's mind. I realise this is a tough challenge, but where possible I like to encourage my children to seek out difference and celebrate it. I love how English photographer Brock Elbank has celebrated the diversity of freckled individuals with vivid and refined portraits in his project called freckles for example. Visit www.mrelbank.com to see his work. We need to teach our children to celebrate difference as much as we can to change this tribal mindset that everyone should be the same and fit a particular formula.

49. People have different beliefs about where we go when we die, and often children are moulded in their beliefs by their family. This question is best asked when there is an atmosphere of openness for all religious beliefs and opinions about spirituality. See this question as a wonderful opportunity to listen to a child's response straight from their heart or soul. They may come up with some enlightening and fresh ideas!

Note: Adults often form their ideas about death because they are fearful of it and either want to avoid the idea or create a methodology which makes it all seem 'ok'. This topic can be such an interesting debate. My request is that you are all accepting of the different views in the group, that you are intrigued and respectful of everyone's ideas and see it as an exploration of possibilities. As after all, none of us really knows what happens once we die...

50. Help your child to remember a time maybe at nursery or school, where they were allowed to create freely with paint or crayons. Then ask them to imagine a wall that they were allowed to cover with colour and see what they come up with. Children should love this as anything that is potentially mucky is fun!

Note: Graffiti is a wonderfully expressive art form now embellishing our streets. It allows freedom of expression for beauty and also for communicating a political, social or economic message to society. Imagine if you were given a rainbow selection of spray paints and allowed to tell your story through paint for everyone to see. Expression through art is powerful. It taps into our subconscious and surprising things can emerge. You could actually do this as an exercise with the family. It's great fun if you sit in a large circle with a large piece of paper in the middle, a pile of crayons at the side, play some music and set a timer so the aim is to fill the paper with colour and pattern. You will be amazed at what you will collectively produce! You could of course do this exercise on a wall if you have one large enough that you don't mind being painted on! Go on, create your own 'Family Graffiti Art'!

51. **You might need to ask this question and then give people time to 'mull it over' - it's quite a biggie! Children will most likely come up with some innocent, purely intuitive answers, so however fun or serious let the ideas flow.**

Note: Children are likely to be influenced by the other answers in the group so be aware of that..you may like to let them go first if they feel ready.

We used this question in a family gathering and I was astonished at how brilliantly my teenage son critiqued my answer. Under normal circumstances he doesn't migrate towards academic subjects or intellectual discussion but this proved he is capable of so much more than I first thought. I really did get to see another side to him and it has consequently helped us establish which subjects he might want to take at college - so a significant realisation. This is an example of how 'Gathering Insights' can really help in a practical way - it can open your eyes to see elements of your closest ones which could normally hide under the radar.

I offered up the idea that everyone in the world was born into the world equal. Equal wealth, equal health, equal everything. My son quickly pointed out that it is human nature to strive to be different, to compete and that this is actually what persists our race. Nature requires that balance and order is met by 'survival of the fittest' for example. I soon realised that although my idealistic answer was based in good intent, it maybe wasn't realistic and viable in today's world. This then lead on to an in-depth discussion about how culture or even the natural laws that govern our world could be changed and what consequences that might have.

So, you will no doubt find a good deal of discussion and debate arising from this question. It's a great opportunity to discuss morals, economic trends, and philosophise why current affairs occur and how they influence our world.

52. This may seem a little morbid at first, but the only real certainty in life is in fact that we will all at some point die. How that happens, and what happens to what we call our 'Soul' is not known by anyone. However, what we can do is project forward and think about what we hope to hear people talking about when we are no longer in this world. Children may find this a strange concept to think about as they live in the moment and really don't start to think about their mortality at a young age, but it's a great way to get them more comfortable with the idea of death. Many of us live in denial about it and many of us distract ourselves so we don't have to think about it. But, it's actually a really good way to focus on the life that you are living right now.

Note: Years ago, I read a book by Stephen Covey called the '7 Habits of Highly Effective People'. I've never forgotten the exercise he suggests we do, and to this day I find it useful to return to the exercise, seeing that we all continuously change and evolve. Stephen suggests that you imagine your own funeral and you hear your Eulogy being read out. This exercise focuses the mind on what really matters to you - it helps you identify what the point of your life really is. After thinking about what might be said in your Eulogy, you may like to take it a step further and write your own Eulogy. This can then be a piece of reflective writing that you can come back to and use as a check list to make sure your life is progressing in alignment with what you hope you will become at the end of your wonderful, adventurous lifetime!

I'd love to hear your stories, so if you would like to share some of the experiences you have with your children, friends and family when using these questions, please do share a tweet using #gatheringinsights

4. Laughter Is The Best Medicine!

Why is Laughter and Smiling so good for us?

Think for a moment and take yourself back to a time when you last laughed out loud from deep inside your belly. Can you remember how it felt? Something comes alive inside doesn't it?

The times when I remember laughing and smiling seem to connect me with a genuine authentic part of myself and I experience a lift inside my chest which permeates to other parts of me. This, I suppose, is what people then see emanate through into my eyes, and ultimately into my aura. It doesn't end there... when I smile, I notice others smile too...it's a bit like a yawn, it's infectious! I've even noticed when I've smiled about something while I'm out and about, and a stranger has caught my personal moment; they can't help but connect with the uplifting energy in me also. They may not know what I'm smiling about but there is a 'knowing', as if it reminds them of the same feeling they have had when something has humoured them. It spreads like a germinating seed inside and they show a little smile too...not just on their lips but a glint in their eyes.

Isn't this a wonderful thing? It doesn't cost anything and yet the simple act of smiling or laughing can spread so much joy.

Ever noticed how children are often happier than adults? They have a light energy about them, curious, easy going, free and full of joy. I bet they laugh hundreds of times a day, but as adults' our lives tend to get more serious, and we laugh less frequently. By finding opportunities for humour and more laughter we can improve our emotional health, strengthen relationships, find greater happiness and even add years to our life expectancy!

From a physical point of view, laughter actually strengthens your immune system, boosts mood, diminishes pain, and protects you from the potentially damaging effects of stress. Scientists have researched what smiling and laughter actually do inside our bodies and how our endocrine system reacts in response. A study in Norway found that people with a strong sense of humour outlived those who don't laugh as much. The difference was particularly notable for those fighting cancer.

Physically, a good hearty laugh is said to relieve physical tension and the effects of stress, leaving your muscles relaxed for up to 45 minutes after. It also decreases the stress hormones our bodies produce in response to fight or flight situations. Furthermore, it increases the production of immune cells and infection fighting antibodies, hence increasing our capacity to fight disease. Laughter also triggers the release of the body's natural feel-good chemicals (Endorphins). These clever chemicals promote an overall sense of well-being, they help to bring us back to a place of harmony and balance in our body and may even help relieve pain. Because laughter often requires us to use internal muscles, particularly in the torso and chest area, the action of laughing can help improve the function of blood vessels, increasing blood flow to the heart which can help keep this crucial muscle at optimum efficiency. Finally, laughter diffuses the weight of anger and frustration. Have you ever noticed how people with a good sense of humour seem able to glide through life more easily? They use laughter and humour to gain perspective on life and allow niggles to dissipate and slide away, like water off a duck's back! Keeping negative emotions held within our body restricts the flow of natural energy, starving our organs so they become stagnant and less efficient functionally. So, encouraging joyous energy can help our organs and internal systems flow and function with ease. Try feeling sad, anxious or angry when you are smiling or laughing... it's impossible!

Mentally, laughter can mean you improve efficiency whether that's in relation to your job, teamwork, or home life. Because it reduces stress and tension it consequently increases focus, clarity and problem solving. Without the distraction of stress, you are able to concentrate on the task at hand and also free up your mental energy to find solutions to problems that you may have missed before. This increases your efficiency in tasks and ultimately increases confidence because you are able to achieve your goals. Mood raises with this sense of achievement, which in turn raises self-confidence and ultimately fosters increased self esteem - pivotal for all aspects of living in a social and interactive world. With this new heightened confidence, new opportunities and challenges feel exciting and the potential for new successes increase...you are able to start fulfilling your dreams.

Socially, laughter has many benefits. We are social animals and in our busy lives we often forget the importance of connection and collaboration. A humorous perspective creates psychological distance, which can help people avoid feeling overwhelmed and diffuse conflict. In doing so it also draws you closer to others, encourages problem solving, collaboration and support, which ultimately enriches all aspects of interpersonal relationships. Personal relationships are nourished by positivity - laughter is one the most effective tools for keeping relationships fresh and exciting. Sharing laughter brings joy, vitality and resilience to our intimate partnerships. Laughter unites people during times of change, challenge and conflict. It does this by triggering positive feeling and fostering emotional connection. When we laugh with one another, a positive bond is created as we have managed to share a perspective and find common ground. This common ground helps to make us feel part of a whole, (not alone or in isolation) consequently building trust.

Laughter doesn't need to be clever, or well-rehearsed; simply spending time with friends and family and laughing about the simple things in life is enough to make a profound difference to any gathering of people. You can't enjoy a laugh with other people unless you take the time to truly engage with them. This is why 'Gathering Insights' is the perfect tool to start this interactive process. When you care enough about someone to switch off your phone, and really connect face to face, ask questions and listen to their responses a whole new world of potential opens up. Here is a summary of the Physical, Mental and Social benefits of laughter and some suggestions of how we can incorporate more joy in our lives.

Physical Benefits:
Boosts Immunity
Lowers Stress Hormones
Relaxes Muscle Tension
Increases Heart Efficiency
Decreases Pain

Mental Health Benefits:
Decreases Anxiety and Tension
Relieves Stress
Improves Mood
Increases Motivation and Zest for Life
Strengthens Resilience
Increases Focus and Goal Orientation

Social Benefits:
Strengthens Relationships
Enhances Teamwork
Helps Defuse Conflict
Promotes Group Bonding and Collaboration
Increases Self Awareness

We can all foster more joy and laughter in our lives. Here are some suggestions:

1. Smiling at everyone you see! - they may think you're a bit bonkers, but they won't be able to stop themselves smiling back. It's the best free gift you can give everyone!

2. Gratitude - every morning wake and make a mental (or paper) list of everything you are grateful for. This could be as simple as running water, a hot shower, the sunshine etc. You'll be amazed how much wonder there is already in your life when you look for it.

3. Follow Laughter - when you hear someone laugh, move towards it, even ask 'What's Funny?' or turn and look and smile back. Recognise the part of you that knows how that person feels. Grow that warm feeling inside because you too know what laughter and joy is.

4. Befriend Fun People - funny, positive people are wonderful to be around, they are like magnets for positivity, synchronicity and prosperity. They are masters at finding the funny side in the things that happen in everyday life. They are keen observers - this is how many comedians write their material for performances. They watch people and find humour in all the little absurd things we do!

5. Train Your Playful Heart - Remember being a child? Playful, Curious and Fearless? Make it your mission to do something new every month which scares you a little... in a good way... something that you're curious about maybe and watch how it raises your enthusiasm for life!

6. Gather Insights - one of the 52 questions in this book is 'What is the funniest thing that ever happened to you?'. So this is a perfect opportunity to share your funny story, laugh and spread joy! I remember the first time I played 'Gathering Insights' with my family and we ended up falling about with laughter, bellies aching when my Son told us a story about his pants (I won't say anymore!). That evening we left the table lighter, brighter and I had some great material to share at my Son's future 18th Birthday!

My hope is that by using this book you can invite more opportunity to laugh into your gatherings. The questions will certainly encourage disclosure and reveal surprises! So remember not to take yourself too seriously. The happiest people are the ones who can laugh at themselves and all the mad unpredictability of life!

5. A Problem Shared Is A Problem Halved

Why is Talking good for us?

We all know that talking a problem through with a confidant is very helpful. The saying 'A problem shared is a problem halved' is so true and I think, if we're honest, it's helpful to all of us even if we are introverted or extroverted. I remember a distinct moment during my holistic training when I was practising crystal therapy and a friend of mine (who was also a therapist) agreed to be my test client. I was using crystals strategically placed in her aura to help release negative emotion or stagnant energy. We were both familiar with this process and had already experienced how powerful these crystals or 'tools' were in releasing not only emotions but also thought patterns or unhelpful mental programming. We were expecting the crystals to do all the work (as they probably would have done) but my client started to share and feedback what she was experiencing while the crystals were placed in her aura; she started to relate memories from the past, and at that same moment we both sensed a strong energy change in the room while she talked through her emotions using words. The crystals which were placed around her body may well have amplified our own sensory reaction, so this was an excellent learning experience, because everything we felt change did so vividly and with such clarity. As she spoke of her past experiences we could literally feel the energy in the room and around her aura dissipate. We both looked at each other and said 'Gosh did you feel that? As we've been discussing your feelings, the energy has literally been transformed and released!'.

This was a wonderfully clear and informative experience for us both. We literally sensed the energy change when her words were shared out loud, and then we moved on, completing the crystal technique I was practicing, while acknowledging the fruits of our labour. We suspected the power in this learning experience was also to do with the expedient manner we acknowledged and then moved on, without dwelling or reenacting what had happened...why was this?

Now I know from my own personal experience, simply speaking to counsellors can certainly help to 'relieve' anxiety about situations in our lives. Often counsellors will give practical advice on what can assist in the re-programming of painful memories or experiences and also give us an objective view of ourselves. They are trained to help us identify where the root cause of a problem may lie and then support and guide us to become more aware, so we can then take responsibility and ultimately re-programme ourselves, healing ourselves.

However, I also believe the process of sharing words can, if over indulged, actually have an opposing negative effect. Counsellors have told me that some clients have actually become entrenched in a perpetual loop of sharing and talking. This then becomes a dependant relationship between the client and therapist and can ultimately mean the client ends up reinforcing old memories and experiences as opposed to releasing them for healing. The counsellor is of course trained to be aware of this potential pit fall, and if doing their job correctly, will make the client aware of this behaviour and guide them to take responsibility and move on, through and past this 'barrier' or 'wall'. This of course can take time, and this is where I would express a word of caution. Talking is a powerful healing modality, BUT it must be met with timely responsibility as to avoid the reinforcement of the original pain or negative experience being shared. We must be aware we ALL have tendencies to enjoy attention and can sometimes use talking and sharing as a crutch which ultimately can anchor us in the past.

So, talk with your closest, talk with your friends and confidantes and acknowledge and praise the release you feel deep inside you. Be mindful of the time you spend talking over the same issues, use that as a signal to your highest self to take responsibility and move on to pastures new, relinquishing the past behind you. Talk consciously with the commitment to yourself to heal in the present, freeing yourself for your future and all the potential it holds. Finally offer this powerful talking modality to those dear to you but encourage them to take responsibility early on in the emotional transaction, for the good of both of you.

This book is designed so that you ask questions in a group and explore responses, hopefully using active listening and emotional intelligence to support the release of ideas and emotions in your group or gathering. The pace of this book will help you not to dwell or reinforce, but instead explore and move on, unfolding the treasures among you and gathering precious insights to increase awareness and understanding. Use your wonderful ability to talk wisely and you will start to really experience the power of sharing with words in a conscious and responsible manner.

6. Listen Twice As Much As You Speak

Research shows that on average women use up to 20,000 words a day as opposed to the meagre 7,000 by men. Either way, that's a lot of words! How many do you think you use?

What is Active Listening?

If someone was to ask you 'have you heard what I've just said?' Then it's likely you will say yes...but have you really heard? Have you really understood what they are trying to get across to you?

Active listening is different to 'just listening or hearing'. We might think it's about hearing what the person has said and then being able to reflect back what they have said to us; and yes this is a good practice, as you may come to realise that in fact it's quite hard to reflect back accurately! This is the first sign that actually you didn't take it all in! However, on top of this potential to accurately reflect what a person has said to you, you really should be looking for other subtle signs as well. Active listening includes nonverbal messages. This is where a person will use body language (movement in any part of the body) in conjunction with their words. If we take the time to really look and listen at the same time, then the feedback we get will be so much richer in context and only then really give us the true picture of what they are saying and describing.

Simple techniques can demonstrate this. You can ask someone to say something to you from another room where you can't see them. You will of course hear the words they use (and in fact because you can't see them, you will probably work a little harder to remember what they say). But then when you ask them to say those same words in the same room as you, you will hopefully notice how much more information you receive in the form of body language which makes the communication so much more meaningful. I will discuss the importance of visual cues later on in the book, but for now let's focus on how we can get better at really hearing accurately.

Who listens best?

Interestingly, it's thought that people who are visually impaired will often gain more accurate hearing because their other senses (we have 5 main senses: seeing, hearing, smelling, touch and taste) will develop further to compensate for the decline in sight.

Research studies have been performed to test this theory. Their findings reveal that actually only those who lost their sight early in life (as children) really showed a significant increase in the ability to decipher between different pitched sounds compared to those who have normal sight. Those people who lost their sight later in life showed very little improvement overall. This research suggests that the brain's capacity to reorganise itself early in life means we can increase our hearing capability if there is reason to do so.

What can we do differently?

Evolution requires all animals, including humans, to adapt to their environments so they have a better chance of survival and consequently so their genetic make up can be passed on to future generations. So we can deduce from this fact that we humans are also designed to fine tune our bodies to adapt to changing environmental situations - isn't that clever! But how much do we maximise this potential? If we're honest most of us live our lives in our comfort zone, doing what we know and how we to do it. But because humans have conscious choice, how about if you were able to test your senses and practise - choose to make an advancement? There is no doubt in my mind that your body would adapt and improve to the next level.

We can see this skill in athletes who train their minds to visualise the high jump or 100 metres say, before they actually perform it. Brain experts believe and have proven that if we use intention and visualisation (imagination) ahead of actually doing a certain thing then we can start to grow new neural pathways in the brain, strengthening this existing skill or indeed creating a new one. Neural pathways are much like roads, they lead to a destination (or goal). Some are main roads, used frequently by vehicles so they become known to the user, and others are less travelled, smaller pathways off from the main dual carriage way or motorway. It is these smaller roads we need to fortify with our imagination thereby evolving these smaller roads into dual carriageways. This is how we can potentially change our thoughts, behaviours and actions from our childhood programming into new, more healthy actions in adulthood. Yes, it takes time, discipline and great effort to do this, but it is possible.

In my next chapter I discuss how animals have adapted to their environments by increasing their hearing capacity. We too could do this if we choose. Wouldn't it be great if we taught listening skills in schools from a young age! We could all become highly tuned to the sounds in our environment, much like an Owl!

How can we improve?

So back to listening...on a practical level there are a few things we can test to see how well we are hearing what the other person says. I like the analogy of a dart board. Use these 'ring targets' (on the next page) when you are having a discussion, and when you want to check everyone has understood you or you want to make sure you have explained something clearly enough; during a meeting where a clear understanding of set targets is essential or during times of conflict where you need to make sure everyone is on common ground and in agreement with a way forward. It's also particularly useful when talking about feelings as it encourages the person on the receiving end to empathise with what you are saying or adjust accordingly if they don't get their interpretation right the first time.

I usually start by explaining how I feel about something or sharing an idea, and then I say: 'if you were to put that in your own words what would it sound like?'; or

'So I know I've explained it clearly, what did you hear me say'; or 'Can you repeat that back to me so we're on the same page please?'.

Be aware that some people may be reticent at first as they may think you're checking up on them, but with regular use they will see how good it is to get a clear understanding of each other and eventually you will notice the whole family or team is using the technique! I'm always amazed at how most of the time I've not hit the bullseye or even the inner ring. So I have another go after, asking questions for clarification. Then on my second go it's much more accurate and furthermore the other person feels good because they can see I've taken the time to really understand what they were saying. Hence, this dart board technique has proven to be a really good relationship builder.

The Dart Board Technique

1. **Bullseye**: You reflect back to the person getting your interpretation 100% correct, but also building onto their original statement making it even more meaningful (and they confirm this - they find the extra things you've said helpful builds too). So you score 110%

2. **Inner Ring**: You reflect back to the person getting your interpretation >90% accurate (they confirm it feels you have pretty much fully understood them).

3. **Middle Ring**: You reflect back to the person getting your interpretation >75% accurate (they feel understood well enough but there's room for improvement).

4. **Outer Ring**: You reflect back to the person getting your interpretation 50% accurate or less (they feel you've missed the point! So further clarification is required - you need to ask questions and try again!).

You can use it both ways…you can instigate testing the dart board if you are the one who made the statement first or you can offer up your interpretation if the other person was talking first. It really doesn't matter, but either way it will start to spread a really good, proactive communication habit amongst friends, family and work colleagues. I find this process particularly valuable when I am communicating with my children because it's a great way to check that they've actually listened to my instructions! I get a value back so feel more confident it's sunk in (if they get a low score I explain again and repeat the process until I'm satisfied with a bullseye or inner ring rating) then everyone is on the same page, no ambiguity - great! This is particularly valuable with teenagers!

My second proposal for improved listening skills is aimed at your relationship with yourself and the world around you, so more of an internal practice. When was the last time you sat in a quiet room, with no television, radio, music, distractions and you just listened? I suspect it was a long, long time ago. I encourage you to try this as you'll be amazed at the subtle sounds you are able to pick up. It becomes a mediative experience as while you start to really listen…you slow down, you become more present of you, your body, your heart beat, your breathing and then how those sounds relate to the sounds around you both near and far.

I know people who have decided to make this active listening technique part of their morning routine. They pop their alarm on 30 minutes earlier and make the decision to sit and listen to the world around them before switching any distractions on. It means you are starting your day on your own terms; and most importantly, it teaches you to listen to what your body needs. Only then can we really self heal (because we've listened to what we need that day); learn (because we give ourselves time to reflect and ponder); evolve (because we start to make conscious decisions about where we want to put our intention and how we use our imagination to make new pathways leading to our Soul purpose. There's one for you to ponder!

So how about tomorrow you get up a little earlier, even if it's 10 minutes and you sit and listen. You could even promise yourself to do this once or twice a week. Who knows, you may even start to enjoy it and end up doing it every morning. Start bite size and work up and remember in order to create a new habit you need to be realistic and persevere - they say it takes 21 days to form a habit. I also find it helps to link a new habit with an existing one. So maybe you always make a cup of coffee in the morning? So still do this, but sit with your coffee in silence instead of checking email or flicking through the newspaper. Enjoy the space for you and see what you can hear! After all I believe if we all listened twice as much as we spoke the world would be a much more understanding place.

When you play 'Gathering Insights' with your family or friends you can use your listening skills and watch and sense. A whole new world of perception and interpretation will open up in front you!

7. Train Your Owl Ears
...or should I say moth ears?

If you decide to take some time out to actively listen more, as suggested in the previous chapter, you will start to realise how clever our ears really are. We of course use hearing to evade danger, communicate with everything around us and talk to the community of people we share our lives with every day. In order to do this the human ear is a complex organ, but there are actually only three main bones and three muscles which function together to receive, amplify and transmit sound from the ear drum to the inner ear. These 3 bones are called the ossicles and individually are named the malleus, incus and stapes. The average hearing range for a human is between 20 Hz to 20 kHz but there are many animals who have better hearing than that of humans!

Owls rely on their sharp sight and their hearing to prey at night. Most species of owls have crooked ears; one placed slightly more forward and higher than the other, which allows them to pin point exactly where a sound is coming from. This means they can capture their prey more accurately - usually small animals moving around in the dark. We may assume that owls have the best hearing in the animal kingdom but actually cats top them. They have an average hearing range of 45 - 64 kHz and their ears are also mechanically impressive. A human ear consists of three muscles and three bones to amplify and transmit sound, whereas each cat's ear consists of around 32 muscles allowing them to rotate their ears 180 degrees giving them full peripheral hearing.

Dogs are not quite so impressive but they are still more effective at hearing small sounds compared to humans, that's why they can hear you arriving home before you've opened the front door!

Dolphins, much like bats are able to use echolocation as part of their hearing repertoire. They emit high pitched squeaking sounds which bounce off of objects, and the vibrations created travel back to the lower jaw of the dolphin giving the animal a 'sound map' of what might be coming up ahead.

Rats exhibit ultrasound hearing (sounds that are too high for humans to pick up). Whereas pigeons can hear infrasound (sounds that are much lower than a human can hear). With the average pigeon being able to hear sounds as low as 0.5 Hz, they can detect distant storms, earthquakes and even volcanic eruptions! With their exceptional hearing ability and their navigational skills they are named the best navigators in the world.

Finally, however, the moth takes first prize for hearing. The evolution of the moth's hearing may be due to it's need to evade the threat of their main predator, the bat. Moths have the ability to hear a higher frequency than bats, allowing them to escape before they are eaten!

So, can we improve our hearing to contest the moth? Maybe not, but we can certainly improve it with practise. Many experts recommend practising both filtering techniques and sound finding techniques. I'm sure you're aware of the problem at home when people all talk at the same time, someone has the TV on, and someone else is asking you a question! With age it can become more difficult to differentiate between these noises, but if we consciously focus on one noise at a time, we can develop the skills to filter out the other (maybe less important) noise. This is a skill that can be quite useful, particularly if you live in a family with extravert, enthusiastic children!

Auditory experts also suggest the practise of consciously listening for different sounds in different environments to see how many frequencies of sound you can hear. As mentioned in the previous chapter this can become a meditative experience that both helps to calm the mind (because you are focusing on something other than your thoughts) and increase hearing efficiency. You can choose to do this either in a quiet place (maybe first thing in your garden before everyone has woken) and sense the subtle sounds around you and far away. Or, you can practise this in a busier place like when you are visiting the shopping mall. Sit and see how many different sounds you can decipher! The world is a myriad of subtle sounds that we miss 90% of the time.

8. The Power of Words

I'm sure we've all had experiences when words have hurt us, in fact they often feel more painful than physical wounds. Why is this?

Words consist of vibration and sound. These vibrations (or certain frequencies) resonate with objects and subject matter in our world to create the very reality that surrounds us. Words are the creator; the creator of our universe and cosmos, our lives, our reality. We use words as a way of communicating, they are sound vibrations which when received can instantly conjure thoughts in our minds and once thoughts are produced, so too follow emotions. When these thoughts are generated in our minds and mulled over and over they gain energy, particularly when held within our minds for lengths of time without resolution or release; and then they start producing corresponding emotions deep within our psyche.

These emotions are often translated by our body as a fight or flight response, the release of stress hormones or alternatively as positive endorphins. These emotive reactions in our body have a direct effect on how the body shapes itself and continues to go about it's important daily functions. If the negative emotions created in response to words from others are not released or resolved, the body will manifest a physical ailment; almost like an indicator or warning sign to the person so they can tell something is not working properly in the body. Interestingly we all think of disease as a bad thing, but it's actually the body's way of signalling to us that something is out of alignment, prompting us to change behaviours or situations in our lives so we can come back into harmony again. It's our body's clever way of telling us we have dis-ease with something. In an ideal world, we would all identify the potential harm at the outset, but because we have forgotten to really listen to our bodies we often carry on regardless and then notice months or years later that we have a more significant health problem that is rooted in an unresolved mental thought pattern from years back.

Many well known physiologists have written about the cause and effect of words and thoughts on the body in relation to dis-ease. Louise Hay has written extensive books on this subject and in many, offers an index of symptoms and emotional causes to help people diagnose why they have particular ailments and the emotional root cause linked to the dis-ease in the body. She suggests using mantras (words organised in a positive format) to alleviate the pain associated with the words that may have formed negative thought patterns in the first place. Other healing modalities can be used to heal the thoughts and emotions which are causing the dis-ease such as Reiki, Homeopathy, Kinesiology etc. The trick is to find the right therapy that you best respond to, as everyone is different. Different ailments may also react better to certain therapies, but the key is first to notice the dis-ease and then do something about it; preferably where you drill down to find the root cause, instead of throwing tablets at the problem! It is far better to heal the wound instead of putting a plaster over it time and time again. The main point is we need to learn to HEAR ourselves better.

So, the very fact that words can have such a significant effect on our minds, emotions and bodies raises the issue of what can we do to safeguard ourselves against the negative thoughts or judgements of others and how do we make sure our own language is energetically clean?

As with all things it's about awareness at the start. Our minds are often left to run free in our heads creating all sorts of stories about other people and ourselves. We need to learn when to listen to this mind chatter, and when to realise it's an unhealthy over use of imagination based on insecurities, or sabotage programmes.

Secondly, we need to train ourselves to decide what we will listen to and what we'll let pass by. Practised meditation can help with this, but it's not for everyone. I personally find doing activities that bring me back to a place of calm using inward contemplation (to gain an appreciation of the world around me) really helps. When I am creating my art for example, I quickly become aware of my mind chatter and then I can start to decipher which things are useful and healthy for me, and which are not.

Then I make a decision. It's usually based on these two questions:

Is this train of thought based in fear? Or is this train of thought based in love?

If you drill down, you will realise there are only really these two basic principles at play with everything in our lives. Most of our insecurities, feeling of anger or jealousy are based in fear. Fear that we are not good enough; fear of uncertainty, fear that we will fail etc etc. So, choose the train of thought that is based in love, openness, curiosity, playfulness, freedom and compassion. Then you will feel the burden of your thoughts lift before you know it, you are on the track to releasing your constraining patterns of behaviour. I have used this technique many times and I've been astonished at how as soon as I consciously choose the path of love, it's as if a dark cloud has lifted from me. Try it, you'll be surprised…but of course you also need to be fully open to this process, believe in your power of choice and you also need to WANT to change your thoughts for the better.

This latter exercise helps with managing our inner chatter, often produced by things that other people have said to us. But what can we do to increase our awareness of the words that come out of our own mouths and are projected on to others? My first suggestion is that we learn to speak less and listen far more. In Chapter 6 I talk about the importance of active listening and how it can enrich our lives and be a catalyst for personal awareness and emotional intelligence. When you start to really listen to people you suddenly realise how skilled you can be at 'reading' them. Intuition is an innate ability we all hold, but we have become lazy over the ages and forgotten how to use it. Listening is a doorway into this fragrant world of intuition. One where you start hearing the words people use, the tone of those words and the body language that is expressed along with them. You may even start to notice an energy shift as people talk about different things - almost like a transparent veil that ebbs and flows around them - their aura literally tells a story if you are willing to really observe, and I will talk more about this in the final chapter of this book.

So, once you are better at listening to others, you will realise it's less important to say as much. This then allows you the space in your inner world to choose more carefully what you do decide to share. I like to use a simple tool as a filter for what I do and don't decide to say. Simply, I ask myself:

Is what I'm about to say 1. True 2. Kind 3. Necessary?

You will realise very quickly that it's actually quite difficult to satisfy all three questions with a yes! This is mainly because we very rarely know something is absolutely true, it's often based in conjecture! Sometimes what we're about to say isn't kind either. If we really analyse our motives we often say things to make ourselves feel better, draw comparisons or judge people, often in very subtle ways. Much of what we do end up saying is actually not necessary. When we think about the consequences of what we might say, it would change our answer. We also tend to say things that satisfy our own Ego, and actually it really adds very little value to the other person.

I have been practising using this tool for a good while now and I can't say I remember it all the time, in fact probably less than 50% of the time, but, I'm improving and we all need to start somewhere. I recommend you start using it and observe how you communicate with words. It's a humbling process, one where I've had to recoil a few times and admit I was wrong and wish I could take back my unnecessary waffling!

This leads me on to the subject of gossip. An unnecessary indulgence that many of us take part in. Essentially, this is another form of harming with words, because a person doesn't have to be there to be affected by the things we say. It may seem appealing to talk about others, and it may even seem like a vehicle for connection between two people sharing views but gossip holds no positive benefit. It only adds energy to conjecture. When you think about it, there is very little that we can be 100% sure is TRUE in what people say. Therefore most of what we comment about is based on perception. Everyone has a different perspective and so conversation is really based on a mixture of perspectives interpreted in different ways by different people.

Our world is based in energy, what we put out in the world is reflected back to us. Therefore, we must learn to discipline ourselves to speak in a way that conveys respect, gentleness and humility. Even though you may feel compelled to act as a result of any passing feeling, thought or impression, pause and ask whether this is really kind or necessary. People often randomly dump the contents of their mind without regard and when we talk about trivial matters, gossiping about others our attention is wasted on hearsay. Instead we could put our words to good use and project kindness, compliments, and positive spins on what we perceive. When we speak we should speak with mindfulness. Ironically the very fact that our minds are so full makes it hard to filter what we should or should not say, but if we start small we can train our minds to become full of much kinder words to share with the world.

This leads me to the final point. What would you do if you realised after using the pointers above that you've actually caused harm with your words? Firstly, well done for being honest with yourself…and now it's time to be honest with the other person and say sorry. The most humbling and freeing thing you can do is to be so honest that you start to scare yourself.

Thich Nhat Hanh, a contemporary Buddhist monk tells how speaking the truth in a loving way is so necessary, even when we are communicating differences or during disagreements. He says, "We must be 'lovingly honest'; we must discipline ourselves to speak in a manner that conveys respect, gentleness, and humility".

So start today, choose to become conscious of the words you set free from your mouth, question whether they are true, kind or necessary and start to select words instead that breed loving kindness.

The times when I have said sorry (often to my children if I've lost my temper) I have felt a weight lift from me, but more importantly I have watched their faces soften and their hearts fill. We really do underestimate the power of sincere apology when admitting we have made a mistake. It requires courage, a willingness to be vulnerable and what is most wonderful, is that it shows the other person how authentic we are when we apologise. That in itself then signals to them that they can do the same for others. You end up sewing the seed for honesty, and it can grow in a very humbling and powerful way. I've noticed this change in behaviour with my own children; they too have learnt to admit when they are wrong because I as their parent, am not too afraid to admit that I make mistakes too and say sorry.

Yehuda Berg said "words have energy and power with the ability to help, to heal, to hinder, to hurt, to harm, to humiliate and to humble". I believe we all have a responsibility to use words more consciously, with integrity and respect for their potential power. We hold the keys to create more compassion, love, and understanding in our families and communities. Choose to use your words as seeds instead of bullets and then through this conscious use of words we can heal ourselves and others.

As a society we have become conditioned to talk about our misfortunes and problems more frequently than the positive things that occur. We take our interpretations of events, people and ourselves and communicate them to the world, hence bringing those very things into existence. We need to realise that we act as human transmission beacons sending out whatever we conjure in our minds. When you say something out loud enough times, your words (and actually even your thoughts) become truth, not only in your own mind, but in the minds of everyone you are saying them to.

So why do we continue to moan and relay our grievances time and time again knowing that this will only distill further negativity? Do you really want to tell yourself and everyone that you know that you are sad/angry/unsuccessful/miserable/bored or whatever you have been complaining about? Particularly now that you understand it is these exact words that are creating the life you live?

Instead, we can take responsibility and begin to consciously choose the words we would like to use to mould our lives in the future. Don't be surprised if there is a time delay - the universe won't be able to adapt straight away (which is why so many people give up with positive thinking strategies); there is a period of adjustment, but after a while you will begin to notice that your newly chosen words start to attract different, more positive things into your life. You may find you attract new friendships which are lighter, people with a more positive attitude (because that is what you are now projecting). You may find opportunities come knocking on your door, and then they lead to further positive experiences. If you follow the rule of communicating anything good in your life, it's a bit like dominos…it will have a knock on effect. This doesn't mean you have to ignore your doubts and difficult times, but choose how you share them, make sure the balance is always skewed to the positive. You can still share openly to those you trust for support during difficult times but do this with discrimination and always remember to fully take ownership for what comes forth from your mouth!

As the creator of your universe you always have choice. So, next time when you catch yourself starting to say something with a negative connotation, pause and reframe it into the positive thing that you would like to manifest in your life instead. For example, rather than saying 'I'm so unhappy in my job' choose to say 'I'm so looking forward to the moment when I have a job I love. I'd really appreciate your help in finding ways I can make this change happen'. Or 'I am so overweight, it really gets me down' and instead say 'I am in the process of becoming healthier and every day I get closer to my ideal weight'.

Regain your control and frame your words of communication so they reflect the kind of world you want to live in. You can also use 'I am' with more determination and self assurance. These two small but incredibly powerful words will define who you are to yourself and everyone around you once spoken out loud (and internally). When you say 'I am fat/lazy/shy/useless' or 'I am beautiful/intelligent/confident' this is the exact truth you are projecting into the world like the broadcasting mast of a telecoms company. The words and intention that you use literally ripple through the universe like radio waves, attracting more of the same frequency.

Some people use positive words and affirmations can be used to start the day and end the day. Many successful entrepreneur's use this technique - because it works! How about you try setting your alarm 10 minutes early each morning so you can rise out of bed, sit quietly on the floor, take a nourishing breath and silently say positive words in your mind about how you would like this new day to be? Start your affirmation using 'I Am' and this will make it even more powerful. It's also really great to focus the mind at the start of the day, and you will notice that you can recall the words you used in the morning at any point in the day, like a positive anchor. You can use this same approach at the end of the day. Before falling asleep, place one hand on your heart and one hand on your solar plexus (middle torso just below where your rib cages meet), breathe calmly and think of three things that were really good about your day. End by sending gratitude for the people, ideas, places and opportunities that you experienced. Gratitude is a hugely powerful tool in positive living. I've even been known to write 'I feel gratitude' on post it notes and strategically place them around the home so whenever I find them, it reminds me to get into the mind space of gratitude, pause for a moment, (remembering where I am in the whole scheme of things), and feel gratitude run through me. The great thing is, when other people in the family find the notes it gives you an excuse to share the exercise with them, and in doing so you are spreading more gratitude!

The final thing I would like to say on this subject is that all these techniques and ideas are great, but they only really work if you firstly want them to, and secondly if you choose to believe. Many people attend positive thinking seminars and workshops hoping that the approach will change their lives. What they don't realise is that:

1. There is a time delay (it's not instant and you have to put the ground work in first);
2. They hold limiting beliefs from the past that will sabotage any positivity;
3. Their fear is greater than their courage.

So if you are prepared to create this new habit to consciously choose your words to build the life you want, make sure you become aware of your limiting beliefs and re-programme them so your efforts are fruitful; persist with the habit for at least 21days in order to fully integrate it; and finally, build your courage! Then you will be on the right path to creating the life you really want to live, breathe and rejoice in.

Remember, your words = your world

So from now on:

1. Choose your words carefully and consciously, phrasing them to represent what you want to attain in life;
2. If you forget and use negative words, retract them in your mind and over lay them with positive affirmations;
3. Give yourself time to implement this new way of communicating to the world, be patient yet disciplined;
4. Always speak from your heart, and spread loving kindness.

En-joy!

9. Visual Cues

While you are 'Gathering Insights' with your family or friends you will start to notice how important body language and voice tone is when noticing peoples' responses to questions. We've already talked about the importance of active listening, sharing, and the power of words. When you put words, tone, body language and mannerisms into the mix all together, only then will you get a complete picture of how that person is really thinking and feeling. Visual cues are an integral part of this communication process, the icing on the cake if you like.

It's likely you've heard the adage that communication is made up of only 7% verbal and 93% non verbal aspects. The non verbal component being made up of body language (55%) and tone of voice (38%). Hence the 7-38-55 rule of communication. This idea or 'rule' has become ingrained in our society as a benchmark for understanding how communication is broken down into its elements, and teaching people how to better decipher what people are REALLY communicating.

In fact, the study which generated this 'rule' is now being contested by many. Professor Mehrabian originally combined the results of just a few studies on the use of specific words that he performed back in 1971 (published in a book called 'Silent Messages'). His results were circulated across mass media in the late 1960s in abbreviated form, hence how people have come to misinterpret their true meaning. Moreover, the fact that the results comprised of just a few studies would not hold validity in this present day.

Speech alone can certainly get the message across as seen in one of the most famous speeches of all time - Abraham Lincoln's "Gettysburg Address." Its 272 words continue to inspire 150 years after they were spoken. No one has the slightest idea of Lincoln's movements or voice tones during this speech so clearly there is great power in the words we potentially use as described in chapter 8.

With all this being said, we intuitively know how useful it can be to see a person talk in front of us. Communication is a complex thing as a speaker's words are only a fraction of their efforts. The pitch and tone of their voice, the speed and rhythm of the spoken word, and the pauses between those words may express more than what is being communicated by the words alone. Furthermore, their bodily gestures, posture, pose and expressions usually convey a tapestry of subtle signals. These non-verbal elements can present a listener with important clues to the speaker's thoughts and feelings and thus substantiate or contradict the speaker's words.

If I'm honest, I'm not worried about the exact figures or proportions we allocate to verbal or non-verbal communication. I KNOW in my bones as I'm sure you do, that all of it is important. It's like painting a picture. You wouldn't choose to just use pencil and line in monochrome if you really wanted to depict all the feeling, atmosphere, and depth in a subject matter. You would use a myriad of colours, shades, textures and tones to convey the true essence of a landscape scene or person, when painting. In fact, as we know a painting can say so much more compared to even a photograph. This is because it includes the artist's interpretation and perspective.

So, let's forget about the absolute numbers but make sure we incorporate the interpretation of body language, voice and tone in our assessment of a person who is communicating with us. Only then can we build an accurate picture and 'Gather Insights' into their true nature.

So, what are some of the most useful cues you can learn from this book to aid your experience of gathering insights? I personally believe the eyes are the windows to the Soul and although the position of legs, arms and body posture also allude to the overall communication style, I believe the eyes are the key.

On this basis I would like to share the significance of eye movements when someone is talking so you too can benefit from this knowledge. Because we usually make eye contact during communication it also makes perfect sense to notice the nuances that occur while someone is retrieving data from their mind. The direction that the eyes take and how pupils dilate or constrict can give us valuable information. Often it can be intimidating if someone 'looks you up and down' for other body cues, so by focusing on the eyes we are able to keep contact in a more discrete and comfortable manner.

Have you ever held a conversation with someone while they are wearing sunglasses and realised how uncomfortable it feels? It's hard to determine their mood or responses because you can't clearly see their eyes isn't it? This proves how naturally we all want to 'read' and respond to the eyes during communication. Personally, it makes me feel really quite uneasy if I can't clearly see their emotions through their eyes, partly because I want to check that what I may be saying is ok with them, or at least be able to 'read' their reactions in response. I much prefer to feel connected to them.

Eye movements correlate with which part of the brain hemisphere or memory bank we are tapping into in order to formulate our response. This is a huge subject, so I will keep things simple for now as my intention is to give you bite size chunks of information that are user friendly for the purpose of this book.

Eye Movements & Interpretation

Generally, the way we process our environment can be displayed through our eyes in the following categories. Looking up means some kind of visual imagery, looking side to side suggests the processing of sound and looking down means they are either self-talking or feeling emotions.

1. Looking Up

If a person looks up while talking, it often suggests they are recalling a time in the past and thinking. For example, if a person is delivering a speech it is likely they will look upwards if they are trying to remember their notes or prepared words. The direction in which they look up will determine whether they are recalling something factual or imagined. This can differ from person to person depending whether they have a preference for left or right handed dominance. Neuro-linguistic Programming (a discipline that looks at at the relationship between neurological processes and language and behaviour) explains that the majority of people are 'normally wired' so will look to the left and up, in order to recall a memory; but occasionally some people are wired in reverse. Instead they make constructed pictures by looking up to the left and look right for recall. Therefore, be careful with this technique if you are trying to decipher if someone is telling the truth or not (fact or fiction)! Test them out first of all by asking them a factual question that you also know to be correct. This will then determine which way they look upwards when recalling fact and then the opposite will be true for when they are constructing an imaginative scenario or constructing an imaginative picture in their mind (or indeed a lie!). Remember that you will be seeing their reaction in reverse if you are sitting opposite to them. So for example a person who looks up and to their left (after testing) (your right) suggests to you (sitting opposite to them) that they are recalling a memory.

Looking up may also be a sign that a person is bored and searching their interior world for information, or memories to entertain themselves with, or they may be using their imagination to construct ideas. Imagine making a shopping list while sitting in a boring meeting, you would probably look up and to the left because you're trying to remember what's in your cupboards at home!

Understand that these guidelines are made in isolation of other body language. Looking up at another person with the head lowered can suggest something very different - this would portray a coy and suggestive style of communication because it combines the lowering of the head in a submissive manner, drawing in the receiver with the intent of attraction. Contrastingly, a lowering of the head with upward gaze can suggest a judgemental approach especially when combined with a frown! So you can see how important it is to consider the whole communication package even though the eyes are a profound element.

2. Looking Down
The way or angle we look at a person can determine whether we are intending to dominate them or become submissive to them. Looking down means we are not looking the other person in the eye, hence we are sending the message that we're not a threat, 'please don't hurt me'. It also suggests that in doing this the other person is dominant, so there is an exchange of power going on. These lowering actions may also indicate guilt, fear, sadness, again other mannerisms must be taken into consideration when determining the exact intention of communication. Arm position, hand positions and stance will all interplay with how a person tilts their head and position their eyes. Looking downwards and to the left can indicate that they are talking to themselves (inner talk), whereas looking downwards and to the right indicates they are connecting with internal emotions. Test this on yourself...if you ask yourself an emotionally charged question such as 'what was the saddest time of my life?', you will feel first hand which way your eyes drop.

3. Looking Sideways
Because our eyes are set in the front of our foreheads, most of our vision is in the horizontal plane. So this suggests that if someone looks sideways they are either purposely looking away from what is in front of them or looking towards something that has taken their interest. A quick glance sideways may purely be to assess a distraction.

As with all animals, we too need to scan our environment for potential danger, risk and hazards, so we may look sideways quickly to assess a distracting sound for instance. However, looking sideways can also indicate irritation, for example if you didn't agree with what the other person has said and internally want to avoid it or disassociate from it.

Looking to the right can indicate they are imagining a sound; as with visual and other movements, this can be reversed for some people so make sure you do a test first to decipher truth or fabrication. Constructed sounds for people wired in reverse might be straight left and recalled sounds may be straight right. So again, remember to test for switching.

Lateral movement from side to side can indicate that a person is uncertain of their response and this may be because they are lying or trying to make things up as they go along. The darting of eyes from side to side may suggest that they are flicking from their memory banks to imagination in an attempt to conjure stories and weave a web of deceit.

It can also suggest that they are conspiring and checking that nobody else is listening or watching. Be cautious again, as eye movements in all directions, sideways and up and down can suggest a manic mind trying to make sense of lots of data in quite a panicked way or having to take in lots of different data at once and trying to make sense of it in the bigger picture. Again, it is imperative that the eye movements are considered as part of the whole communication ensemble, so that other parts of the body are observed and assessed in conjunction.

I hope you can now start to see how complex yet enthralling communication is. There are many aspects at play at any given moment in time when we observe another. If we don't take in the full picture of body language (including eye movements and gestures from all parts of the body) alongside words, tone etc we can misconstrue what the other person is trying to get across to us. We must learn to use the observation of eye movement in conjunction with all the other queues and most important trust our innate ability to intuit what the other person is really saying.

You will be pleased to know that if you are being present with the other person, and really listening and watching, you have (as we all do) this innate ability to 'read' a person. Trust your intuition when looking for all the signals and you will be amazed at how much information is there in front of you being offered up by the other person. As creatures taught to survive in a world full of potential predators and hazards we have innate and primitive capabilities to 'read' other people and animals. This is a truth that we must all look to learn again as it has become dulled over time because we no longer take the time out of our busy distracting lives to be present with those around us. This is how 'Gathering Insights' can be become a conduit for you and your family and friends' self-discovery.

Finally, eye movement can not only help you 'read' and understand the people around you more accurately, it can also act as an aid in your own self development. You can use it to help you think more clearly. When you want to create images, you can look up to the side (depending on your preference for left/right handedness) to accentuate this creative process. When you need to tune in to your feelings you can help the process along by looking down to the right. If you talk to yourself too much, or you may be aware you make yourself sad by looking down often, you can make a conscious effort to place your gaze somewhere else and shift the mental process. Emotions follow thought, so if your eyes are placed in a different receptive position you can in effect change your mood. Again, this is another way of forming and transmuting your own reality as described in chapter 8.

Most of us have habitual ways of thinking and processing information so if you try to move your eyes smoothly around in a circle you may even find places where they stick. These places might hold the key to untapped resources and creative thinking! Who knows what potential is locked within you! The unconscious mind and how it functions is a well of untapped and as yet not fully understood potential. Enjoy being in your body, using it as a tool for self-discovery and helping other's around you to see themselves and others more clearly. I hope this little taster about body language and queues has whetted your appetite!

So based upon what I have discussed, what message do you think the squirrel is sending to you?

If you'd like to know the context in which this photograph was taken and how the squirrel was acting, tweet your question, including hashtag **#gatheringinsights**

10. Aura Intelligence

So far, we've talked about the importance of laughter, sharing and expressing problems, listening actively, the power of words, and significance of visual cues in communication. Did you know there is a wondrous yet invisible force around every living thing that can give additional amazing insights to you and everyone around you?

Each living creature, plant, and even objects have an energy field surrounding them, and this energy field serves to nourish, heal and sustain the functioning of the physical body or entity. It is called the aura and is made up of bands of energy almost like the colour frequencies in a rainbow. By definition, an aura is 'the distinctive atmosphere or quality that seems to surround and be generated by a person, thing, or place'. So even non-living things can give out a type of energy or feeling and manifest an aura. Your aura is the energetic field that emanates from your physical body and indicates your general mood, state, or way of being. It can be consciously adjusted if you are skilled in energy work; for example, you can use intent to inject certain colours into your own aura to maybe boost confidence and increase relaxation. Your aura can also change quickly in response to your environment, the people around you (as their auras may affect yours) and the situations you find yourself in. Stress for example can shrink your aura, while love can expand it and change it's colour. You will also develop different combinations of auric colour over your lifetime as you change and adapt to life experiences. I'm sure you can all recall a time when you were feeling stressed and depleted in energy and then you shared a meal, laughter and joy with a trusted friend. Somehow the transfer of energy between you and your friend 'lightened' your mood and you left the meeting feeling refreshed. This is an example of how other peoples' aura energy can influence our own.

The aura is generated by our mental thought, emotional feelings and spiritual beliefs as a reaction to our internal and external worlds. Because it can be easily influenced by our surroundings, other people's auras and the changing situations we find ourselves in, we may use it to describe a person and the mood they are in at any given moment in time - it is a malleable and transmutable energy reference. I have had my aura photographed several times over the years and each time the colours within it have altered. This shows a progression in my personal development. For example, when I first had my aura captured I had a large area of blue/green to the right-hand side of my aura indicating that healing energies (indicated by the colour green) would be developing in me over the following few years and that I may end up working in a healing role, communicating the healing arts to other people (indicated by the colour blue). I was indeed training in Reiki at that time and had just started developing my intuitive skills, but had no idea that years later I would write a book and offer healing to clients through my own healing consultancy business.

More recently my aura has shown these same colours moving across my aura into the left side with violets, reds and golds inhabiting the top section indicating that I have established a higher connection to self awareness and the spiritual realms. This has taken several years, but my aura has held a record of the transformations that have taken place in my mental, emotional and spiritual development. Some people are even able to see their spirit guides as white entities hovering above their auras in photographs, so their auras even show how a person may be protected and guided in life. Different colours in specific areas can indicate particular changes or qualities or even act as warning signs. A person with black in their aura may be showing signs of depression or holding on to negative beliefs for example.

We all know what if feels like when a charismatic person enters the room. For some 'unseen' reason people turn and look, attracted to the energy they emanate. We commonly use the phrases 'that person is very charismatic' or 'they have a larger than life personality' when actually what we are intuitively picking up on is their strong aura. Such people will have developed a very strong sense of who they are, built self confidence and esteem descriptive of their personality and true nature which literally shines out from their physical body. This auric energy is so confident and congruent with who they are as a person it sends clear signals to us all which we can't help but notice and be attracted to. People like this often 'light up a room' and influence the mood of not just one person but a whole group and may also influence the atmosphere of their environment. Leaders, politicians and people in positions of influence often have these charismatic auras. Think for a moment about the people you know or socialise with. Who is the most charismatic among your friends? Why do you think this is? No doubt there will be underlying reasons why their aura is so influential. Of course, this can work both ways! There are also people who 'drain' other peoples' auras. They are often referred to as emotional vampires or victim personalities who have the opposite effect to people with charisma. Who we choose to spend our time with, can have a great effect on our own auric health. So, when you start to become aware of the auras around you, you can start to make conscious choices about where you place your own energy in relation to others.

On a deeper level, the thoughts, feelings and spiritual beliefs we hold as a result of the experiences we have in life are also reflected in our chakra system. The chakras differ from the aura in that they are more anchored and represent themselves more like a blueprint or network of our true nature, less fluid or quick to respond to external stimuli. That isn't to say they don't change, they do, but in a more integral way, shifting from the effects of more persistent stimuli.

The chakras are vortices or rotating wheels (chakra means wheel in Sanskrit) responsible for allowing etheric energy (auric energy or 'atmosphere' around the physical body) to move in to the physical body and also move out from the physical body. They are doorways of a kind, and are hence responsible for the physical, emotional, mental and spiritual wellbeing of the human form or living creature. The chakras are anchored in place and act as metabolising centres often governing certain specific areas of the body, managing collections of organs and bodily functions. Their healthy functioning is hence vital to the health of the physical body. They also act as conduits for connection to divine energies and altered states of consciousness. While auras can be adjusted based on current mood and intent, your chakras remain more anchored and rooted so it would take a significant change in your life to influence a change in the chakras. However, the chakras can still 'paint a picture' of your life story and current situation. Intuitive healers can use them to ascertain where balance and support is required in order to acquire better health and they often report chakra readings to be more accurate than auric readings. Therapists reading the chakra system can diagnose the current areas of weakness or strength in a person and then make suggestions on how that person may change their lifestyle, hence influencing beneficial changes in the chakras and ultimately the optimum functioning of the physical body.

There are many chakras held within our body often following meridian lines making up a network of energy highways by which the body moves and disperses energy. This is how acupuncture therapists tap into the energy system. The main chakras comprise of seven centres (or wheels of energy) positioned down the central line of our physical body and they all have corresponding colours which hold a relationship with the potential hues seen in the aura as a manifestation surrounding the body. Here is a summary list below.

1.   **Root Chakra**:
         Location: at the pubic bone or base of the torso
         Synonymous with: security, abundance, tribal culture 'we'
         Colour: Red
         Element: Earth

2. **Sacral Chakra**:
    Location: in the lower belly or womb area
    Synonymous with: sexuality, sensuality, intimate
    relationships, creativity, 1:1 encounters, you and I.
    Colour: Orange
    Element: Water

3. **Solar Plexus**:
    Location: the diaphragm where the two rib cages
    separate
    Synonymous with: self esteem, personal power,
    confidence, self worth, 'I'.
    Colour: Yellow
    Element: Fire

4. **Heart Chakra**:
    Location: in the mid chest region, parallel to the heart
    Synonymous with: unconditional love, self love,
    forgiveness, compassion, 'the healing centre'.
    Colour: Pale Green or Pink
    Element: Air

5. **Throat Chakra**:
    Location: in the dip where throat meets collar bone
    Synonymous with: communication, expression, creativity,
    choice, self will, discipline, accountability for decisions.
    Colour: Mid Blue

6. **Third Eye Chakra**:
    Location: slightly above the mid eye brow point in the
    forehead
    Synonymous with: mind, intuition, insight, awareness,
    mental thought, future intent, management of illusions.
    Colour: Indigo or Purple

7. **Crown Chakra**:
    Location: Top of head
    Synonymous with: spirituality, the divine, angelic realm,
    cosmic, oneness, union, 'the grace bank account'.
    Colour: White or Violet

Use this analogy to help describe and assimilate the aura and chakra system in your mind: imagine the chakra system as the planet earth and the atmosphere surrounding it as the etheric aura. The chakras are the continents, each with their own individual landscape and culture. They are anchored in a particular form, unless significant change forces them to adapt such as an earthquake occurring which consequently moves the earth's crust into a different formation. Each continent has a relationship with the others and there are ways and means of travelling between them. The atmosphere surrounding the planet is influenced by the environmental impact of the physical planet beneath it and represents the aura. It is more fluid and changeable compared to the physical planet below, influenced by the weather systems that move within it, changing hourly and daily. The weather is a mirror of the underlying integrity of the planet below (as seen with the deterioration of our ozone layer) and depending on how well we look after our continents and living bio-systems this too reflects on the health and authenticity of the aura above. The true nature of the planet can only be known by looking at the whole, but the underlying physical planet is the real source of the aura (i.e. the chakras determine our aura output). The whole (planet and atmosphere) live within a wider existence in the solar system and universe. Each planet, moon and the stars has an influence on the others (as do our chakras and auras with other people).

I love how this analogy amalgamates all the elements of the energy management system in one familiar territory. Hopefully you are starting to see how this energy management system plays such a vital role in our holistic health as both individuals and a whole human race within a cosmos yet to be fully discovered. There is so much we are yet to understand about how the micro relates to the macro in our bodies and universe. As I learn more, I only realise how little I know and I find that so very exciting!

I hope you can also see the value in being able to sense and read a person's chakras and aura. Imagine if we could see people as they really are, without having to interpret body language for example. In his book 'The Third Eye (1986) T. Lobsang Rampa describes spying on visiting Chinese dignitaries at the monastery. He had been training himself to see auras for a while and came to use this skill to understand the real motives and true feelings of people, as opposed to purely listening to their words in communication. He comments "As I looked at them from my place of concealment, I observed the shimmering of their auras, the opalescent sheen, shot with murky red, the turgid swirling of hate-filled thoughts. Bands and striations of colour, unpleasant colours, not clear, pure shades of lighter thought, but the unwholesome, contaminated hues of those whose life forces are devoted to materialism and evil doing. Their speech was fair, but their thoughts were foul".

Like Rampa, by training our sixth sense (or intuition) we can become more in tune with our innate ability to read peoples' energy. This is turn may actually end up being the most accurate sense of a person even though it is to many invisible. If you are interested in learning more about this topic and how you can fine tune your intuitive skills further, I would recommend you consider training in Reiki. This is an ancient healing art which requires a person to learn to sense auras and chakras and ultimately balance the energies to increase health and wellness. Reiki literally means 'universal life force'. It is not spiritual healing, it is the ability to channel the natural healing force that exists around all living things and as a Reiki therapist you purely offer yourself up as a conduit for this pure and cleansing energy. When this energy flows from therapist to client the chakra system can re-align itself back into harmonious balance which in turn supports the body's natural ability to self heal. If only we were taught this wonderful healing modality in school. We would all have our very own first aid kit with us at all times! Maybe one day Reiki and energy management will become second nature (as it once was) just like cleaning our teeth in the morning!

Summary

I hope by now you have indulged in time spent with your loved ones, whether friends or family, dipped into a good few of the 52 questions and started to experience how they can open up a whole new world of insights. Hopefully you have been intrigued enough to delve a little further and learn about the power of words, ascertain how well you actually listen or hear what others say, and notice the body language or cues we are given.

Maybe you've even opened a new window in your mind and started to ask questions about the relationship between body, emotion, mind and Soul. You have witnessed how intention is formed within us and projected from us as human 'beacons'. You may have even started to change and adapt some of your behaviours and habits in response to 'Gathering Insights'. If this is the case, then my goal for this first book has been met.

A seed may have been planted in your 'garden of awareness', so from here I hope you keep it watered and nourished as otherwise you will never know what beauty may flourish forth.

Finally, I offer some plant food for your garden - a few suggestions of further reading and research to keep your compost rich and nutritious. These are a collection of resources which I have found useful and that I feel may 'hit a spot'. Obviously as life evolves some of these resources will become outdated but I hope they at least offer a doorway into your curiosity to learn and evolve and seek more understanding.

Please do share your insights and revelations with the wider community by using #gatheringinsights in social media and if you feel friends would enjoy the book please do spread the word! I'd also love to hear about your stories so do message me at sonya@bristolreiki-healingarts.co.uk and tell me all about your experiences using this book.

With love,
Sonya X

Bibliography & Resources

Q5. Coaching & Visualisation
Book: Whitmore, J. Coaching for Performance - Growing People, Performance and Purpose.
Nicholas Brealey Publishing; 4 edition (4 Jun. 2009)

Q7. Mother Nature & Society
YouTube Video: Nature Is Speaking – Julia Roberts is Mother Nature I Conservation International (CI) (1:59 minutes)
Youtube Video: Gaia The Big Mother (Film 48:50 minutes)
www.worldcentric.org stats on the degradation of planet Earth
YouTube Video: The Third Industrial Revolution: A Radical New Sharing Economy (1:45 minutes)

Q8. Thinking and Feeling
Myers Briggs Type Indicator by Isabel Briggs Myers
www.myersbriggs.org
1:1 Personality testing www.bristolreiki-healingarts.co.uk
YouTube Video: Myers Briggs MBTI Part 4 of 6 - Thinking and Feeling (10.33 minutes)

Q11. Planet Mars & Elon Musk
www.spacex.com
YouTube Video: Elon Musk wants to go to Mars. His reusable Falcon Heavy rocket is now one leap closer (5:08 minutes)

Q13. Keeping Imagination Alive
www.paulocoelhoblog.com Einstein Quotes to live by
YouTube Video: (Full Speech) Jim Carrey's Commencement Address at the 2014 MUM Graduation (26:09 minutes)

Q14. Colours & The Chakra System
www.colour-affects.co.uk/how-it-works
www.blog.mindvalley.com/7-chakras/
www.myss.com/free-resources/chakras-your-energetic-being/
Book: Mc Geough, M. (2013) A Beginner's Guide to the Chakras.
CreateSpace Independent Publishing Platform (8 Nov. 2013)

Q16. Gratitude
Book: Trier, E. (2014) The Gratitude Project: A Year Of Saying Thank You To The People Who Changed My Life. CreateSpace Independent Publishing Platform; 2 edition (7 April 2014)
Podcast: Theatre of The Mind - 'The Importance of Gratitude' Interview with Dr. Robert A Emmons
YouTube Video: BBC Documentary Breadline Kids 2018 (58:42 minutes)
YouTube Video: The End of Poverty 2011 www.confutatis.org (1hr 44:33 minutes)

Q17. Message in a Bottle (perspective on your life)
Book: Covey, S R. (1999) The 7 Habits of Highly Effective People. Simon and Schuster; Reprinted Edition edition (4 Jan. 2004). In particular read habit 2 'Begin With The End In Mind'.

Q18. Motivation in Life
Book: Maslow A H. (2013) A Theory of Human Motivation. Wilder Publications (28 Sept. 2013)
www.simplypsychology.org/maslow.html

Q19. Intuition
Youtube Video: 'How to Understand Your Intuitive Nature - Reflections Seminar 1' by Caroline Myss 2014 (1hr 30:17 minutes)
Podcast: Theatre of The Mind - 'Practical Intuition' Interview with Laura Day 2006
www.mindbodygreen.com/0-17693/18-ways-to-strengthen-your-intuition.html

Q27. Soul Families
Book: De Angelis, B. Secrets About Life Every Woman Should Know - Ten Principles For total Spiritual And Emotional Fulfilment. Thorsons (1 Aug. 2009). Read secret no.8 and p223 in particular.

Q28. Spirit Animals
www.mindbodygreen.com/articles/how-to-find-your-spirit-animal
For Fun, Try this Quiz: www.quizony.com/what-is-your-spirit-animal/27.html

Q29. Conquering Fear

Book: Jeffers, S. Feel the Fear and Do it Anyway 2017. Vermilion (2 Feb. 2017)

Book: Millman, D. The Way of The Peaceful Warrior - The Book That Changes Lives.

H J Kramer; 20Anniversary Ed edition (1 Sept. 2000)

Film: Peaceful Warrior 2006 with Nick Nolte and Amy Smart

Film: Evan Almighty (there's some wonderful quotes and snippets relating to how we can overcome fear in this film and it's great for all ages to watch).

Q34. Elevator Pitch

www.wikihow.com/Develop-Your-Personal-Elevator-Pitch

YouTube Video: 'The Best Elevator Pitch' Vanessa Van Edwards 2014 (7:09 minutes)

www.themuse.com/advice/the-15minute-method-to-writing-an-unforgettable-elevator-speech

Q35. Avatars

Film: Avatar 2009 by James Cameron

https://www.ananda.org/yogapedia/avatar/

Q40. Love Languages

Book: Chapman, G. The Five Love Languages 2015.

Moody Press; First edition (20 Feb. 2015)

Q44. Auras

Youtube Video: What is an Aura? | Sadhguru (8.03 minutes)

Youtube Video: Caroline Myss The Energetics of Healing 1998 Part 2 (1hr 29:25 minutes)

Book: Brennan, B. Hands of Light: A Guide to Healing Through the Human Energy Field. Bantam; Reissue edition (23 Mar. 2011)

Q46. Time and Perception

Book: Taylor, S. Making Time: Why Time Seems to Pass at Different Speeds and How to Control it 2008. Icon Books Ltd; Original edition (3 July 2008)

YouTube Video: Time and the brain: the illusion of now | Hinze Hogendoorn | TEDxUtrechtUniversity (16.07 minutes)

Gratitude

I am so very grateful to all the people who have enriched my life so far and helped me to learn lessons, both challenging and joyful. Without this learning I would not be the person I am today and hence able to share little pieces of wisdom and knowledge. So to those who I know, and those I don't, but who have all crossed my path and played a part in this continuing adventure…thank you.

To those I know intimately as friends and family; my greatest thanks goes to you wise souls…to my son Max and my daughter Macy who are wiser souls than me. To my two step daughters Hannah and Ellie who inject a modern and energetic twist to ideas and have helped test out questions.

To my dear life partner and companion Neil who has helped me realise my true potential; a gift only a true soulmate can offer.

To the talented Samantha Clift who reproduced my eye for the front cover! If you would like to commission Sam for photo realistic art, visit her website www.samanthacliftart.co.uk.

To David Ford who used his own ingenious creative eye to produce a cohesive and impactful design for the cover.

To Gina Schofield and Nicola Johnston for their attention to detail; you were both so generous with your time.

Namaste
'The light in me sees the light in you'

11105272R00072

Printed in Great Britain
by Amazon